アスコム
英語マスター
シリーズ

CDブック

1日5分で
英語脳をつくる
音読ドリル

デイビッド・セイン
David A. Thayne

アスコム

はじめに

35万人が体験し、大反響だった英語脳をつくる特別メソッド。

デイビッド・セイン
David A. Thayne

→ 英語がスラスラわかるようになる特別トレーニング

　私はこれまで25年以上、数万人に及ぶ日本人に英語を教えてきました。その中で私が気がついたのは、「どうしても英語が上達しない」と悩む生徒が、実にたくさんいるということです。

　日本人の英語がなかなか上達しない理由の1つは、英語を英語のまま理解できないことにあります。英語と日本語とでは構造がまったく異なるというのに、英語をいったん日本語に訳してから理解しようとするので、スラスラ英語を理解できないのです。そこで私が開発したのが、英語を英語のまま理解することができるようになる、「英語脳」をつくるトレーニングです。

　この方法を試した生徒さんは、実際、ぐんぐん英語力を伸ばしています。「**やった人は必ず伸びる**」これが私の実感です。

　英語の学習方法に迷っているあなた、一定レベルに達したもののそこから伸び悩んでいるあなた、まずは15日間、そしてさらに15日間、ぜひこのトレーニングをやってみてください。**1カ月で、英語がぐんと上達したことを実感できるでしょう。**この本には、もっと英語力を高めたい方のためにさらに15日間分の「もっと上達するトレーニング」をおまけにつけました。1冊を終えるころには、想像以上の効果に驚かれることでしょう！

英語脳をつくるトレーニングの特徴

音読 → 音読で英語を効率的にインプット

英語の上達を阻む大きな原因の1つは、英語のインプット不足。英語力アップの決め手は、とにかくたくさんの英語を効率的に脳にインプットすること。音読は、まさにうってつけの方法です。声と同時に耳も使うことで、英語をダブルでインプットできるからです。また、音読には、自分の弱点が明確になる、という特徴もあります。スラスラ読めない部分は理解不足だったり、会話でうまく言えない部分だということ。その部分にアンダーラインを引いたりして、繰り返し練習するのもいい学習方法です。

マーキング → マーキングで構文の理解を深める

マーキングは目・耳以外に、手も使う方法。少しでも多くの器官を使いながら、ある単語を目印にして音読することで、英語の構文がより理解できるようになり、また集中力や学習効果もぐんと高まります。

繰り返し → 繰り返しで単語を確実に身につける

英語学習継続の妨げになる要因の1つに、「新しい表現や単語を覚えてもすぐに忘れてしまう」ことがあります。けれど「忘れた」ことは「進歩がない」こととは違います。すぐに思い出せなくても、確実に脳に蓄積されています。あと何度か繰り返せば、完全に身につくところまできています。

1日5分、15日間の継続 → 毎日少しずつ無理なく続ける

学習には集中力が必要。けれど人間が物事に集中できるのは5分が限界。無理に長時間学習しても効率は上がりませんし、続けること自体が難しくなります。1日5分をまず15日間続けてみてください。毎日少しずつ継続することがポイントです。15日間終わったら、さらに15日間続けてみましょう。

CONTENTS

02 はじめに

06 本書の使い方

10 音読の効果

12 音読と書き取りの活用法

14 音読ドリルの効果を実感!

16 付録CDの使い方

17	1st Step	**15日間トレーニング1**
48	コラム	数字の読み方
49	2st Step	**15日間トレーニング2**
80	コラム	話の流れを見抜くキーワード
81	おまけ	**もっと上達するトレーニング**

本書の使い方

みなさんはこれから、それぞれの英文を、
1日5回、計3日間にわたって繰り返し音読するトレーニングを行います。

→ ドリルの構造

まず、ボールペンまたはサインペンを用意してください。

では、実際に英文サンプルを見ながら、トレーニング方法を説明します。

> He's a smart **dog** and a good **companion**. When someone comes to the **door**, he barks, but he stops when I tell him it's okay. I leave him at **home** when I go to work and he doesn't seem to mind.

これを見ると、英文の中である特定の単語が色付けされています。注意深く見ると、「名詞」のキーワードに色がついていることがわかります。この「名詞」に着目しながら英文を読んでいってください。**品詞を意識しながら単語をマーキングすることで、英語の構文がより理解しやすくなります。**

それでは、P7の要領にしたがって、ドリルをスタートしてください。

→ 1日5分、音読トレーニングの進め方

1回目 まずは何も考えず、そのまま音読します。音読1回の目標時間は約1分間。これを以下の要領にしたがって5回繰り返すので、「1日5分」の学習ということになります。

↓

2回目 色のついた単語を○で囲みながら音読します。
He's a smart ⓓⓞⓖ and a good ⓒⓞⓜⓟⓐⓝⓘⓞⓝ When someone comes to the ⓓⓞⓞⓡ, he barks, but he stops when I tell him it's okay. I leave him at ⓗⓞⓜⓔ when I go to work and he doesn't seem to mind.

↓

3回目 色のついた単語に斜線を引きながら音読します。
He's a smart ⓓⓞⓖ and a good ⓒⓞⓜⓟⓐⓝⓘⓞⓝ When someone comes to the ⓓⓞⓞⓡ, he barks, but he stops when I tell him it's okay. I leave him at ⓗⓞⓜⓔ when I go to work and he doesn't seem to mind.

↓

4回目 色のついた単語に、今度は逆の方向から斜線を引きながら音読します。
He's a smart ⓓⓞⓖ and a good ⓒⓞⓜⓟⓐⓝⓘⓞⓝ When someone comes to the ⓓⓞⓞⓡ, he barks, but he stops when I tell him it's okay. I leave him at ⓗⓞⓜⓔ when I go to work and he doesn't seem to mind.

↓

5回目 色のついた単語を完全に塗りつぶしながら音読します。
He's a smart ■■■ and a good ■■■■■■■■■ When someone comes to the ■■■■, he barks, but he stops when I tell him it's okay. I leave him at ■■■■ when I go to work and he doesn't seem to mind.

→ ドリルの使い方

　1回音読するたびに、ページ下にある「英文読解度」の欄に、自分が英文の内容を何パーセントくらい理解できたか、点数をつけていきましょう。「自分で感じたままの点数」をつけていけばOKです。1日目は名詞に着目。5回繰り返したら、1日目のトレーニングは終了です。

　次に2日目の英文を見ると、今度は同じ英文の主な動詞が色付けされているのがわかります。つまり、今度は動詞に着目しながら、1日目と同じ要領で5回音読するというわけです。3日目の英文では、主な形容詞・副詞に着目しながら5回音読していきましょう。

　4ページ目には、何も色付けしていない英文を載せていますので、自由に使ってください。コピーして何回も使ってみてください。

　5ページ目には「さらに英語をスラスラ読むポイント」を掲載しています。それぞれの英文のポイントや語句の説明、日本語訳が載っています。毎日5回目のトレーニングが終わった後に、このページを読むようにすると、英文の理解がぐっと深まります。ただし、もし、1回目の英文読解度が50％未満だった場合は、先にこちらを読むことをおすすめします。

　本書では、このような15日間トレーニングを2セット行います。ちょうど1カ月分のトレーニングができるようになっています。また「このトレーニング法をもう少し続けて、もっとしっかり身につけたい」という方のために、おまけでさらに5つの英文を掲載しました。ぜひ活用してみてください。

　付録のCDは、発音を確かめたり、ディクテーションに使ったり、リスニングの練習に使ったりなど、どんどん活用してみてください（付録のCDの使い方は16ページ参照）。

　1カ月をかけて、10ユニットの英文を読み終えるころ、みなさんの頭の中には、英語を英語のまま理解できる「英語脳」の回路ができあがっていることでしょう。

　それでは、さっそく始めましょう！

※品詞の色付けは、主な単語にのみ行われています。このトレーニングの目的は、品詞を区分することではなく、単語を目印にして、音読を楽しく、効果的に行うことにあります。細かな文法にとらわれすぎないで、「音読」することに重点を置くことで、英語力がアップします。
※それぞれ6ページ目には日本語訳も掲載していますが、できるだけ日本語訳を見ないでトレーニングすることが英語力をアップさせるコツです。

1日目 → 名詞に注目して音読！
1日5回繰り返し音読。毎回理解度を％で記録します。

2日目 → 動詞に注目して音読！
1日5回繰り返し音読。毎回理解度を％で記録します。

3日目 → 形容詞・副詞に注目して音読！
1日5回繰り返し音読。毎回理解度を％で記録します。

1つの英文を3つの違った視点で、3日間にわたって繰り返し音読します。これを1ユニットとして、1セット15日間。2セット続けると、英語脳ができあがってきます！

脳科学でも実証済み！
脳科学者・中野信子先生が教えてくれる
音読の効果

音読を継続すると、脳が鍛えられ、記憶力が高まり、
効率的に英語が身につきます。

→ 英語と日本語は脳の回路が違う

　日本人の多くは英語が苦手と言われています。その理由は多々ありますが、脳科学から見ると、**日本語と英語の構造上の違いから生じる、脳の回路の違い**によるものが大きいと言うことができます。
　日本語は文字の形を読取り、視覚からその意味をイメージすることができる文字言語です。文字とビジュアルイメージが直結しています。
　それに対して**英語は、文字の形自体は重要ではなく、音声が重視される音声言語**です。見た文字を一度、音に置き換えないとイメージできないのです。
　この「文字→音」への変換作業には英語回路が使われます。この英語回路、誰しもが持ち合わせていますが、日本語では使われることがないため、ほとんどの人がいわば眠った状態にあります。
　ですから、**英語を習得するにはまずこの英語回路を機能させることから始め**てみましょう。

→ 音読は英語回路を鍛えます

　では、眠っている英語回路をどう鍛えればいいのでしょうか。それにはまず、**英語を聞くことから始めます**。その際、文字を同時に目で追うことが重要になります。ビジュアルからサウンドイメージに変換することに慣れることこそ、英語回路の働きを活性化させるのです。
　文字も最初はただのアルファベットの羅列にしか見えないかもしれません。けれども、音と合わせることにより、次第に単語となり、さらにはセンテンスとなり、徐々にその範囲は広がっていくはずです。**文字という記号が音によっ**

て結びついたときこそ、**英語回路がしっかりと働いている証**となります。

英語を聞いて文字を見るのは、脳へのインプットになります。しかし、ただ聞くだけでは覚えることにはつながりません。ここから**英語を脳へ定着させるにはアウトプットが必要**になります。アウトプットしてはじめて、記憶することができるのです。

この**アウトプットの作業こそが「音読」**になります。音を聞く→文字を見る→音読する。これを繰り返すことにより、英語を覚えられるようになります。

→ 英語学習は筋トレと同じ

また、**英語の学習は筋力トレーニング**のようなものです。**基本的には「聞く→音読→書き取り」を繰り返すことにより、英語回路を鍛えていきます。**

腹筋や背筋のトレーニングをするのと同じで、目と耳と口、そして手を動かす筋トレと割り切り、継続させることを心掛けましょう。

また、筋力トレーニングには準備体操が必要ですが、英語においても学習前に洋楽を聴いたりすると頭がほぐれます。英語の音はもちろんですが、音楽のリズムにより、いわば英語回路のストレッチを行うことができます。

また、時間があるときは吹き替えではない洋画を見るのもおすすめです。英語以外の視覚的要素で何を言っているのかがおおよそ判断できるので、準備運動にもってこいです。

最後に学習とは失敗の繰り返しです。知らない単語が出てきてもおそれずに、**とにかく続けていくことが何よりも重要**です。

中野信子 Nobuko Nakano

脳科学者

東京大学工学部応用化学科卒業。東京大学大学院医学系研究科脳神経医学専攻博士課程修了・医学博士。2008年より、フランス原子力庁サクレー研究所で、博士研究員として勤務。2009年からは、世界上位2%のIQ所有者のみ入会を許される「MENSA」に所属。2010年に帰国し、研究・執筆を中心に活動中。近著に『世界で通用する人がいつもやっていること』(アスコム)がある。ポスト茂木健一郎とも呼ばれ、学習法だけではなく、音楽と脳、恋愛と脳、コスプレと脳など従来にない脳の分析を得意とする。

©森モーリー鷹博

脳を活性化させて
英語をもっと効率的に身につける

音読と書き取りの活用法

音読で脳をウォーミングアップ、書き取りと合わせればより脳は活性化し、学習効果がぐんと高まります。

→ 音読で脳をウォーミングアップ

　「音」を聞くことは脳科学的に見ても、非常に重要な要素です。
　人が情報を得るときには五感（視覚、聴覚、触覚、味覚、嗅覚）を働かせます。特にその中でも、目と耳は重要な役割を果たします。脳への情報伝達は、目による視覚野と耳による聴覚野が働くのですが、聴覚野による伝達の方が早く、視覚野のおよそ3分の1程度で情報を処理できるのです。
　例えば、緊急時に避難などを促す情報などは、音で「危険です」と知らせたほうが、より早く脳に伝わり、すぐに行動することができます。**音は脳へより早く情報を伝え処理するので、より脳を刺激し、働かせるので、音が脳を活性化していると言える**のです。
　また、**コミュニケーションの基本は音によるやり取り**です。動物は鳴き声で、人間はそれを言語として持ち合わせています。ですから、人は耳から入る音の情報を処理する能力に長けているのです。
　特に**英語は音声主体の言語として、この音による能力をフルに活用します**。だからこそ、まずは「音を聞く」ことが必要になるのです。
　音読の際には、音の変化に特に注目しましょう。

→ 書き取りでワーキングメモリーを鍛える

英語をより効率的に覚えるためには**ワーキングメモリーを拡大させることがポイント**になります。ワーキングメモリーとは脳で情報を一時的に溜めておく場所のことです。例えるなら、台所で使うまな板のようなものでしょうか。まな板が広ければ、たくさんの野菜や果物を置き、調理できるように、ワーキングメモリーも大きければ、たくさんの情報を一度に溜め込むことができる、つまり記憶力そのものがよくなるのです。

これには、音を聞く→文字を見る→音読する、という作業のほかに、ディクテーション、つまり書き取りが効果的です。**音読しながら書き取りを行うことで、インプットとアウトプットが双方向で行われ、ワーキングメモリーが鍛えられます。**

ワーキングメモリーを鍛えるには、聞き取りの音が速いほうが、より脳が刺激され有効です。はじめは遅くてもかまいませんが、徐々にスピードアップしていけば、その分、情報処理能力は高まります。

→ 夜寝る前の英語学習がおすすめです

英語をより効率的に学習するには、夜、特に寝る前に覚えることをおすすめします。

人は新しい情報が入ってくると、古いものは忘れてしまいます。けれども寝る直前に学習したものは、それ以上新しい情報が入ってこないため、寝ている間に記憶として定着しやすいのです。

ですから、**寝る前のまずは5分でもいいので、英語を聞き、音読して、できれば書き取りを行ってみてください。**それを2～3週間、毎日継続することで、英語回路が自分のものとして動いているのが実感できるはずです。英語回路を鍛えることは、マラソンのトレーニングのようなものです。走りもせずに、完走しようと思っても難しいもの。けれども、毎日少しでも走り込んでおけば、いつかは完走できるはずです。

脳科学的に見ても、人により習得の差はありますが、**継続さえすれば、誰でも英語を覚えることはできます。**年齢などは関係ありません。お肌の潤いを保つには、毎日のスキンケアが欠かせないように、英語回路を動かすためには毎日、英語に触れることが大切なのです。

音読ドリルの効果を実感！

1日5分15日間で
オドロキの効果！

いち早く「1日5分で英語脳をつくる音読ドリル」を、2週間体験してもらったモニターさんに、実際、英語力がどのように変わったか、効果や感想を伺いました。

→ 目と耳と口からの英語の刺激で、確実に英語がわかるように！

　口に出して読むことで理解力が高まることを実感しました。最初は5回も読むのかと思っていたのですが、1回目よりも2回目、2回目よりも3回目と確実に理解できるようになっていました。また、手を使うことで一度ポーズが入るのもよかったと思います。流し読みを重ねるだけで理解力がアップするということを知れたのは大きかったです。ついつい訳しながら読んでしまうのですが、複数回流し読みした方が早く、よく理解できるのが実感できました。高校時代以来の英語の音読でしたが、とても楽しかったです。黙読だとついわかった気になってしまいがちですが、音読することで耳からの刺激も入り、わからないところについても理解できるようになりました。

Hiroki さん　34歳男性

英文読解度の変化に注目！

音読ドリルを始める前 **75**%　2週間　音読ドリルを体験した後 **90**%

→ 苦手だった英語に自信がつきました!

　英語が苦手な私には、ちょっと難しかったのですが、頑張って2週間毎日続けました。最初は長い英文に圧倒されていましたが、読んでいくうちに気持ちをこめて読めるようになってきました。読み方がわからない単語は付属のCDを聞いて、発音を確かめてマネをしながら読みました。自分で言うのもなんですが、かなりレベルアップできた気がします。

Amiさん　32歳女性

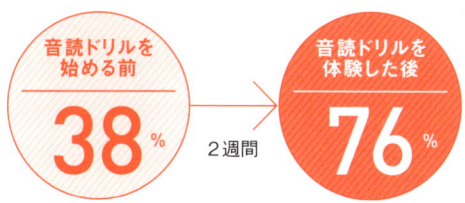

→ 音読ドリルの想像以上の効果にびっくりです!

　もともと英語は好きな方なのですが、流し読みをするくせがあり、わかったつもりでわかっていない、というのが現実でした。音読をすることで、わからない部分や自分の苦手な部分が明らかになって、ちゃんと向き合って調べたり、練習したりすることができました。そのせいか、たった2週間のトレーニングだったのに、自信がついたし、内容もきちんと理解できるようになりました。

Maikoさん　38歳女性

1日5分で英語脳をつくる
音読ドリル
付録CDの使い方

本書には、英文を収録したCD1枚がついています。本書の音読ドリルの発音の確認や、確実に英文が記憶できているかどうかの確認などにお使いください。なるべく5回目の音読が終わった後にCDを聞くようにしてください。どうしても発音に自信がない人は、最初にCDを聞いてから音読をはじめましょう。

収録内容

トラック番号

1〜10　1st Step　15日間トレーニング1
11〜20　2nd Step　15日間トレーニング2
21〜30　おまけ　もっと上達するトレーニング

CDマークの見方

CDイラストとマークについている数字は、CDトラック番号です。各ユニットの英文を収録した音声には、男性と女性の音声の2つのパターンがあります。

1　男性の音声で音読します。
2　女性の音声で音読します。

※本書のCDは、CDプレーヤーでご使用ください（パソコンで使用すると、不具合が生じる場合があります）。

1st Step
15日間トレーニング 1

I need a watchdog to watch my dog.

うちの犬を見張ってくれる番犬がほしい

TRACK 001, TRACK 002

Last year, my **house** got robbed three times while I wasn't at **home**. I was thinking about getting a security **system**, but I got a big German Shepherd instead.

He's a smart **dog** and a good **companion**. When someone comes to the **door**, he barks, but he stops when I tell him it's okay. I leave him at **home** when I go to work and he doesn't seem to mind.

A few months ago, things in my **house** started to go missing. I thought a **robber** was somehow getting into my **house** when I was at **work**. A nice **watch** went missing, and then someone took some **cash**. One day, someone took my **wallet** while I was asleep. I didn't know what to do!

Then one day, I couldn't find my **cell phone**. I thought someone had stolen it too! But then I heard it ring. It was in my dog's **stomach**! I still love him, but maybe he's not so smart. I think I need a **watchdog** to watch my **dog**.

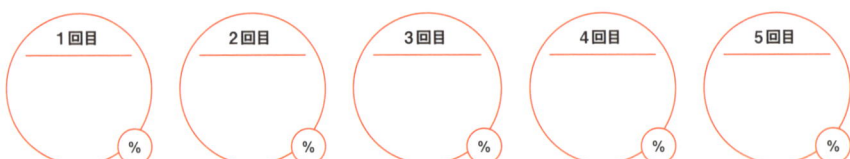

day 2

I need a watchdog to watch my dog.

動詞に注目して音読してください

うちの犬を見張ってくれる番犬がほしい

TRACK 001, TRACK 002

Last year, my house got **robbed** three times while I wasn't at home. I was **thinking** about getting a security system, but I **got** a big German Shepherd instead.

He's a smart dog and a good companion. When someone **comes** to the door, he **barks**, but he **stops** when I **tell** him it's okay. I **leave** him at home when I **go** to work and he doesn't **seem** to mind.

A few months ago, things in my house **started** to go missing. I **thought** a robber was somehow getting into my house when I was at work. A nice watch **went** missing, and then someone **took** some cash. One day, someone **took** my wallet while I was asleep. I didn't **know** what to do!

Then one day, I couldn't **find** my cell phone. I **thought** someone had **stolen** it too! But then I **heard** it ring. It was in my dog's stomach! I still **love** him, but maybe he's not so smart. I **think** I need a watchdog to watch my dog.

英文読解度 （文の内容を何％くらい理解できましたか？　理解度を入れてください）

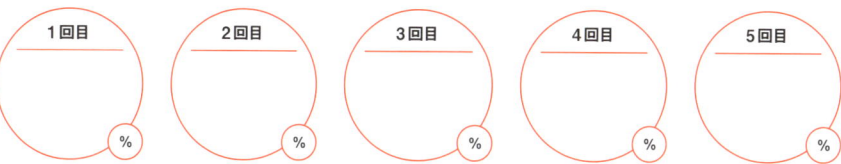

day 3
I need a watchdog to watch my dog.
うちの犬を見張ってくれる番犬がほしい

形容詞・副詞に注目して音読してください

TRACK 001, TRACK 002

Last year, my house got robbed three times while I wasn't at home. I was thinking about getting a security system, but I got a **big** German Shepherd instead.

He's a **smart** dog and a **good** companion. When someone comes to the door, he barks, but he stops when I tell him it's okay. I leave him at home when I go to work and he doesn't seem to mind.

A few months ago, things in **my** house started to go missing. I thought a robber was **somehow** getting into **my** house when I was at work. A **nice** watch went missing, and then someone took **some** cash. One day, someone took my wallet while I was **asleep**. I didn't know what to do!

Then one day, I couldn't find **my** cell phone. I thought someone had stolen it too! But then I heard it ring. It was in **my** dog's stomach! I **still** love him, but maybe he's not so **smart**. I think I need a watchdog to watch **my** dog.

英文読解度 (文の内容を何％くらい理解できましたか？ 理解度を入れてください)

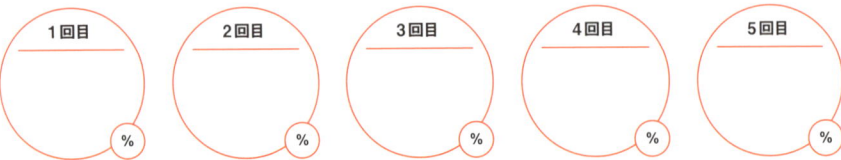

TRACK 001, TRACK 002

I need a watchdog to watch my dog.

うちの犬を見張ってくれる番犬がほしい

コピーして何回も
使ってください

Last year, my house got robbed three times while I wasn't at home. I was thinking about getting a security system, but I got a big German Shepherd instead.

He's a smart dog and a good companion. When someone comes to the door, he barks, but he stops when I tell him it's okay. I leave him at home when I go to work and he doesn't seem to mind.

A few months ago, things in my house started to go missing. I thought a robber was somehow getting into my house when I was at work. A nice watch went missing, and then someone took some cash. One day, someone took my wallet while I was asleep. I didn't know what to do!

Then one day, I couldn't find my cell phone. I thought someone had stolen it too! But then I heard it ring. It was in my dog's stomach! I still love him, but maybe he's not so smart. I think I need a watchdog to watch my dog.

英文読解度 （文の内容を何％くらい理解できましたか？ 理解度を入れてください）

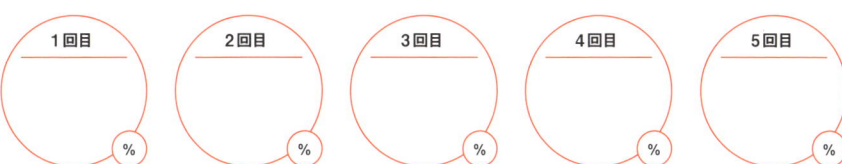

さらに英語をスラスラ読むポイント

get は「ゲットする」だけではない！

受身形「〜される」は <be + 過去分詞> と学校で習いますが、その be の代役となれるのが get。この用法を使いこなすには、動詞の過去分詞形をしっかり覚えましょう！下の①で詳しく！

→ ここに注目

① ... my house got robbed ...（1行目）
<get + 過去分詞> は、<be + 過去分詞> と同じく、「〜される」という意味。rob「(場所) を荒らす、襲う」が過去分詞形 robbed になり、get と使われると、get robbed「荒らされる」となります。get hit by a car は「車にはねられる」、get bitten by a dog は「犬にかまれる」、get scolded は「しかられる」という意味。

② ... I didn't know what to do!（12行目）
what の後に不定詞が続いた形 what to do は「何を〜すればいいか」、「何を〜すべきか」という意味で使われます。know what to do で「何をしたらいいかわかっている」という意味。where や which、how も to 不定詞を続けることができます。what to say「何と言ったらいいか」、where to go「どこに行ったらいいか」、how to get to the station「どう駅に行ったらいいか（駅への行き方）」という言い方があります。

③ ... I heard it ring.（14行目）
hear は <hear + 名詞>「〜が聞こえる」という形のほかに、<hear + 名詞 + do>「〜が〜するのが聞こえる」という形でも使うことができます。ここの it「それ」とは my cell phone「私の携帯電話」のことで、heard it ring は「それ（私の携帯電話）が鳴るのが聞こえた」という意味になります。hear には <hear + 名詞 + doing>「〜が〜しているのが聞こえる」や <hear + 名詞 + done>「〜が〜されるのが聞こえる」という用法もあります。

→ 語句

watchdog：番犬
security system：防犯システム
German Shepherd：ジャーマンシェパード
somehow：何とかして、どうにかして
get into...：〈家や部屋などに〉入る
at work：仕事に出て
go missing：行方不明になる
cell phone：携帯電話

→ 日本語訳

　去年、空き巣に３回入られました。防犯システムを買おうと思っていましたが、代わりに大きなジャーマンシェパードを買いました。
　彼は頭のいい犬であり良き仲間です。ドアのところに人が来ると吠えますが、私が大丈夫だと言うと吠えるのをやめます。仕事に行くときは彼を家に残していきますが、気にしていないようです。
　２、３カ月前のことですが、家のものがなくなるようになったんです。私の仕事中に、泥棒がなんとかして家に入り込んでいるのだと思いました。いい腕時計がなくなり、次に現金が取られました。ある日、睡眠中に財布を取られました。どうしたらいいかわからなくなってしまいました！
　それから、ある日は携帯電話が見つからなかったんです。それも盗まれたと思ったんです！　でも、そのとき、ベルの音が聞こえてきました。うちの犬のおなかの中にあったんです！　今も彼のことが大好きですが、彼はそれほど賢くはないかもしれません。うちの犬を見張ってくれる番犬が必要だと思います。

No more waste!

TRACK 003, TRACK 004

名詞に注目して音読してください

浪費はこれ以上しない！

Do you remember when vegetable **prices** went up last **year**? Well, I decided my **family** would have to eat fewer **vegetables**. But then I read a **book** on how to cut down on **waste**.

One of the things it recommended was to stop making impulse purchases. My **fridge** isn't very big, but I used to buy a lot of raw things like **fish** and **vegetables** just because they were cheap. It may sound silly, but I'd often leave the **things** out until they went bad!

Another thing the **book** recommended was to make a weekly meal **plan**. It can be a **headache** to plan every **meal** of the week, so I just plan ten **meals**. We eat mainly **fish** and **salad** on Mondays, Wednesdays and Fridays. Then on Tuesdays and Thursdays, we eat mostly **chicken**, **vegetables** and seasonal **fruit**. And then on weekends, we eat out.

In this way, we succeed in using up all the perishable **food** in our **refrigerator** before it spoils. It feels like we're eating more **vegetables** than ever now, and saving **money**!

英文読解度 （文の内容を何％くらい理解できましたか？ 理解度を入れてください）

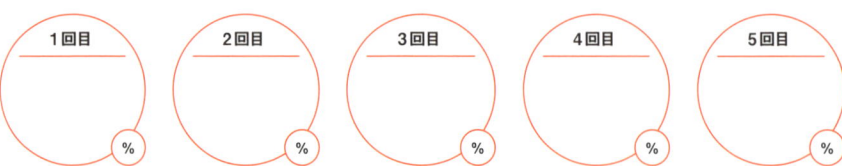

day 5 No more waste!

TRACK 003, TRACK 004

浪費はこれ以上しない！

Do you **remember** when vegetable prices **went** up last year? Well, I **decided** my family would have to **eat** fewer vegetables. But then I **read** a book on how to **cut** down on waste.

One of the things it **recommended** was to stop making impulse purchases. My fridge isn't very big, but I used to **buy** a lot of raw things like fish and vegetables just because they were cheap. It may **sound** silly, but I'd often **leave** the things out until they **went** bad!

Another thing the book recommended was to **make** a weekly meal plan. It can be a headache to **plan** every meal of the week, so I just **plan** ten meals. We **eat** mainly fish and salad on Mondays, Wednesdays and Fridays. Then on Tuesdays and Thursdays, we **eat** mostly chicken, vegetables and seasonal fruit. And then on weekends, we **eat** out.

In this way, we **succeed** in using up all the perishable food in our refrigerator before it **spoils**. It **feels** like we're **eating** more vegetables than ever now, and **saving** money!

英文読解度 (文の内容を何％くらい理解できましたか？ 理解度を入れてください)

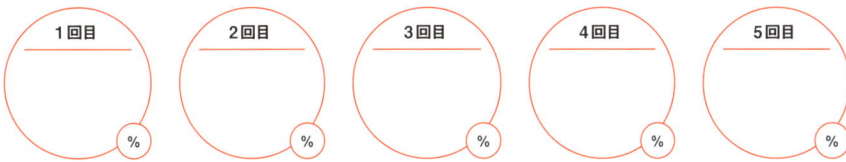

day 6
No more waste!

浪費はこれ以上しない！

Do you remember when vegetable prices went up **last** year? Well, I decided **my** family would have to eat **fewer** vegetables. But then I read a book on how to cut down on waste.

One of the things it recommended was to stop making impulse purchases. **My** fridge isn't very **big**, but I used to buy a lot of **raw** things like fish and vegetables **just** because they were **cheap**. It may sound **silly**, but I'd **often** leave the things out until they went **bad**!

Another thing the book recommended was to make a **weekly** meal plan. It can be a headache to plan **every** meal of the week, so I **just** plan ten meals. We eat **mainly** fish and salad on Mondays, Wednesdays and Fridays. Then on Tuesdays and Thursdays, we eat **mostly** chicken, vegetables and **seasonal** fruit. And then on weekends, we eat out.

In **this** way, we succeed in using up all the **perishable** food in **our** refrigerator before it spoils. It feels like we're eating more vegetables than ever **now**, and saving money!

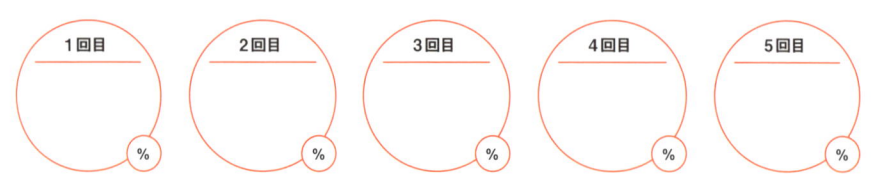

No more waste!

浪費はこれ以上しない！

Do you remember when vegetable prices went up last year? Well, I decided my family would have to eat fewer vegetables. But then I read a book on how to cut down on waste.

One of the things it recommended was to stop making impulse purchases. My fridge isn't very big, but I used to buy a lot of raw things like fish and vegetables just because they were cheap. It may sound silly, but I'd often leave the things out until they went bad!

Another thing the book recommended was to make a weekly meal plan. It can be a headache to plan every meal of the week, so I just plan ten meals. We eat mainly fish and salad on Mondays, Wednesdays and Fridays. Then on Tuesdays and Thursdays, we eat mostly chicken, vegetables and seasonal fruit. And then on weekends, we eat out.

In this way, we succeed in using up all the perishable food in our refrigerator before it spoils. It feels like we're eating more vegetables than ever now, and saving money!

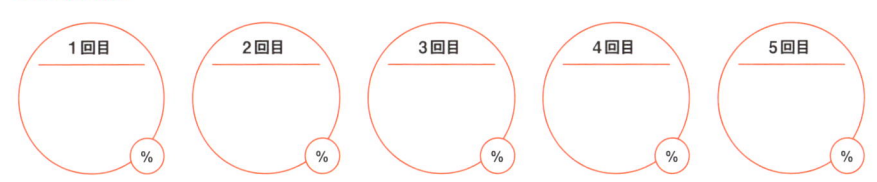

さらに英語をスラスラ読むポイント

makeに「〜をする」という意味が?!

make に「〜をする」という意味があるといっても、play baseball「野球をする」や do the laundry「洗濯をする」が make を使って言い換えられるわけではありません。下の①で詳しく！

→ ここに注目

① ... making impulse purchases.（5行目）
make は動作や行為を表わす名詞を目的語とすると、「〜をする」という意味で使われます。この意味の make と impulse purchase「衝動買い」が組み合わさって、make an impulse purchase「衝動買いをする」となります。make a call「電話をする」や make a speech「演説をする」の make も同様です。

② It may sound silly, but ...（8行目）
<It may sound + 形容詞 + but ...>「〜に聞こえるかもしれないが〜」という前置きをつけることで、どのようなことを次に述べるのか読者に言っておくことができます。silly「ばかげた」「ばかばかしい」という形容詞を使えば、It may sound silly, but ...「ばかばかしく聞こえるかもしれないが〜」となります。may「〜かもしれない」を使えば、断言が避けられます。「奇妙に聞こえるかもしれないが〜」であれば、It may sound strange, but ... と言います。

③ It feels like ...（17行目）
明言を避けるために「〜な気がする」や「〜な感じがする」と言うことがあります。それを It feels like ... と言い表せます。ここの接続詞 like「〜であるかのように」は as if と言い換えができますが、会話ではよく like が用いられます。

→ 語句

cut down on ...：〜を削減する
waste：浪費、空費
fridge：冷蔵庫
headache：困った問題、悩みの種
seasonal：特定の季節だけの
use ... up：〜を使い尽くす
perishable：腐りやすい

→ 日本語訳

　野菜の値段が去年上がったときのことを覚えていますか？ 私は、うちの家族の野菜の量を減らしたほうがいいと考えました。そんなとき、浪費の減らし方が書いてある本を読みました。

　おすすめの1つが衝動買いをやめることでした。うちの冷蔵庫はあまり大きくないのですが、安いというだけで魚や野菜など生ものを大量に買っていました。愚かに聞こえるかもしれませんが、腐ってしまうまで出しっぱなしにすることもよくありました！

　本では、週の献立をつくることもすすめられていました。1週間にとる全食事の献立をつくるのは面倒だから、10食分だけやっています。月・水・金は主に魚とサラダで、火・木は主にチキン、野菜、旬のフルーツ。そして、週末は外食。

　こうして、うちの家族は、冷蔵庫に入っている腐りやすいものはすべて、腐る前に使い切れています。今では、野菜を以前よりも多く食べていたり、倹約していたりする気がします！

day 7

TRACK 005, TRACK 006

A clean home is a happy home.

きれいな家が幸せな家

名詞に注目して音読してください

I tell everyone how much I hate **housecleaning**. That's why I work hard to make it easier. One **thing** I do is have a big cleaning day at the **beginning** of every **season**. I start by dusting, sweeping and vacuuming. Next, I go through each **room** with a **box**. I open up the **closets** and **drawers** to look for things to throw away. If I haven't used something for a long time, it goes in the **box**.

There's one more thing. I like to clean while listening to **music**. I pick out **music** that will motivate and relax me at the same time. It always makes the **job** go a lot faster.

If I do a good **job** cleaning my **house** four times a year, it makes daily **cleaning** a lot easier. It helps me to keep things organized and it makes my **home** much more relaxing. Just between **you** and **me**, I'm looking forward to the next big cleaning day!

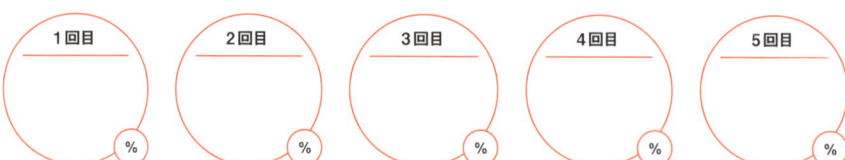

英文読解度 (文の内容を何%くらい理解できましたか？ 理解度を入れてください)

1回目 / 2回目 / 3回目 / 4回目 / 5回目

TRACK 005, TRACK 006

A clean home is a happy home.

きれいな家が幸せな家

I **tell** everyone how much I **hate** housecleaning. That's why I **work** hard to **make** it easier. One thing I do is have a big cleaning day at the beginning of every season. I **start** by dusting, sweeping and vacuuming. Next, I go through each room with a box. I **open** up the closets and drawers to **look** for things to **throw** away. If I haven't **used** something for a long time, it **goes** in the box.

There's one more thing. I like to **clean** while listening to music. I **pick** out music that will **motivate** and **relax** me at the same time. It always **makes** the job go a lot faster.

If I do a good job cleaning my house four times a year, it **makes** daily cleaning a lot easier. It **helps** me to **keep** things organized and it **makes** my home much more relaxing. Just between you and me, I'm **looking** forward to the next big cleaning day!

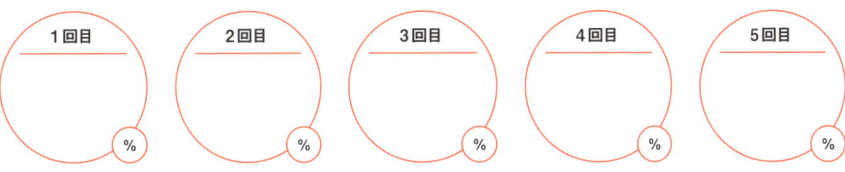

day 9

A clean home is a happy home.

きれいな家が幸せな家

I tell everyone how **much** I hate housecleaning. That's why I work hard to make it **easier**. One thing I do is have a **big** cleaning day at the beginning of **every** season. I start by dusting, sweeping and vacuuming. **Next**, I go through each room with a box. I open up the closets and drawers to look for things to throw away. If I haven't used something for a **long** time, it goes in the box.

There's one **more** thing. I like to clean while listening to music. I pick out music that will motivate and relax me at the **same** time. It **always** makes the job go a lot **faster**.

If I do a **good** job cleaning **my** house four times a year, it makes **daily** cleaning a lot **easier**. It helps me to keep things organized and it makes my home much more **relaxing**. Just between you and me, I'm looking forward to the **next big** cleaning day!

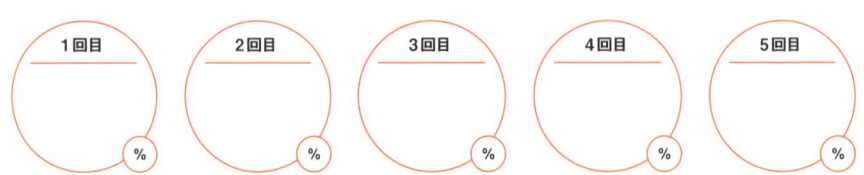

A clean home is a happy home.

きれいな家が幸せな家

I tell everyone how much I hate housecleaning. That's why I work hard to make it easier. One thing I do is have a big cleaning day at the beginning of every season. I start by dusting, sweeping and vacuuming. Next, I go through each room with a box. I open up the closets and drawers to look for things to throw away. If I haven't used something for a long time, it goes in the box.

There's one more thing. I like to clean while listening to music. I pick out music that will motivate and relax me at the same time. It always makes the job go a lot faster.

If I do a good job cleaning my house four times a year, it makes daily cleaning a lot easier. It helps me to keep things organized and it makes my home much more relaxing. Just between you and me, I'm looking forward to the next big cleaning day!

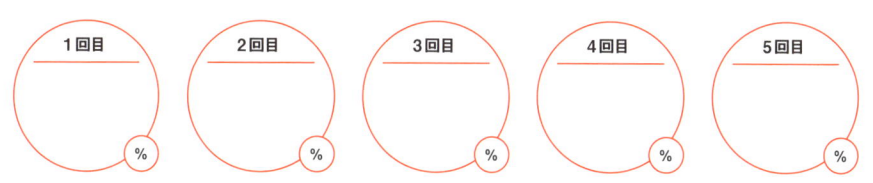

さらに英語をスラスラ読むポイント

between you and me は内緒話の合図!

人から between you and me と言われたら、これから内緒話が始まります。驚いて「あっ！」や「えっ！」と大声を出して周りの人たちに気づかれないように気を付けて！下の③で詳しく！

→ **ここに注目**

① One thing I do ...（2行目）
本文中の One thing I do「私がやっていること」とは、One thing I do to make housecleaning easier「大掃除が楽になるように、私がやっていること」です。One thing I do と言うときは普通、やっていることがたった1つではなく、複数ある場合です。たった1つであるなら、通常 The only thing I do と言います。

② There's one more thing.（8行目）
本文中の There's one more thing.「もう1つある」を詳しく言うと、There's one more thing I do to make housecleaning easier.「大掃除が楽になるように、私がもう1つやっていることがある」になります。There's one more thing. は There's another thing. と言うこともできます。

③ Just between you and me ...（13行目）
(Just) between you and me は「ここだけの話だが」という意味のフレーズです。I tell everyone how much I hate housecleaning.「私は、自分がどれほどの大掃除嫌いなのか、どの人にも言っています」と言っておきながら、実は I'm looking forward to the next big cleaning day!「次の大掃除の日が楽しみなんです！」ということなのです。楽しみにしていることが「ここだけの話」なのです。

→ 語句

housecleaning：大掃除
go through ...：(探し物のために)〈場所など〉をよく調べる
motivate：〈人〉の意欲を起こさせる
... times a year：年に〜回
organize：〜を整理する
look forward to ...：〜を楽しみにして待つ

→ 日本語訳

　私は、自分がどれほどの大掃除嫌いなのか、どの人にも言っています。そういうことなので、大掃除がより楽にできるように頑張っています。やっていることといえば、毎シーズンの頭に大掃除の日を設けていることです。初めにほこりを払って、掃いて、掃除機をかけます。次に、箱を持って各部屋を回ります。クローゼットと引き出しを開けて、捨てるものを探します。ずっと使っていないものがあれば箱に入れます。

　もう1つあります。音楽を聴きながらの掃除が好きなんです。やる気と安らぎを同時にもたらしてくれる音楽を選びます。いつも、作業の進みがぐんと早まるんです。

　家の掃除を年に4度しっかりやると、日々の掃除がうんと楽になります。物が整頓された状態が保たれ、家はさらに落ち着けるところになります。ここだけの話ですが、次の大掃除の日が楽しみなんです！

day 10 I'm sick and tired of mosquitoes!

TRACK 007, TRACK 008

蚊はもうイヤ！

My **house** is right in the middle of a busy **intersection**—an **intersection** for **mosquitoes**. I try to make sure all the windows are closed, but **mosquitoes** still get in.

One Internet site said **garlic** was effective. **Mosquitoes** are attracted to the **smell** of human **sweat**, but when you eat **garlic** and sweat out the smell, they stay away. The site recommended making a garlic **paste** and spreading it on your **skin**. So that's what I did.

For the first time in a long time, I slept like a **baby**. The next **morning**, I went to work and found out I had a new cute **co-worker**. Sadly, it was clear to me that she thought she was being tortured by the strong **smell** of **garlic**. I can't blame her. She must've noticed that the offensive **odor** was from me.

I think I'd better move to Iceland. I hear it's the only **country** in the **world** that doesn't have **mosquitoes**.

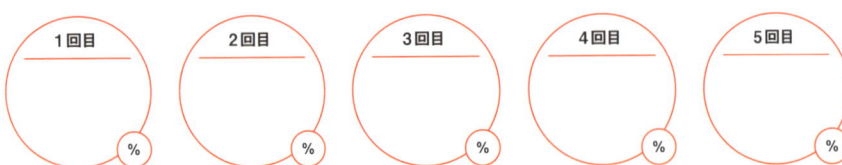

英文読解度（文の内容を何%くらい理解できましたか？ 理解度を入れてください）

1回目 ___ %　2回目 ___ %　3回目 ___ %　4回目 ___ %　5回目 ___ %

day 11
I'm sick and tired of mosquitoes!

TRACK 007, TRACK 008

動詞に注目して音読してください

蚊はもうイヤ！

My house is right in the middle of a busy intersection—an intersection for mosquitoes. I **try** to **make** sure all the windows are closed, but mosquitoes still get in.

One Internet site **said** garlic was effective. Mosquitoes are attracted to the smell of human sweat, but when you **eat** garlic and **sweat** out the smell, they **stay** away. The site recommended **making** a garlic paste and **spreading** it on your skin. So that's what I did.

For the first time in a long time, I **slept** like a baby. The next morning, I **went** to work and **found** out I had a new cute co-worker. Sadly, it was clear to me that she **thought** she was being tortured by the strong smell of garlic. I can't **blame** her. She must've **noticed** that the offensive odor was from me.

I **think** I'd better **move** to Iceland. I **hear** it's the only country in the world that doesn't **have** mosquitoes.

英文読解度 （文の内容を何%くらい理解できましたか？ 理解度を入れてください）

1回目	2回目	3回目	4回目	5回目
%	%	%	%	%

day 12
I'm sick and tired of mosquitoes!

蚊はもうイヤ！

My house is **right** in the middle of a **busy** intersection—an intersection for mosquitoes. I try to make **sure** all the windows are closed, but mosquitoes still get in.

One Internet site said garlic was **effective**. Mosquitoes are **attracted** to the smell of human sweat, but when you eat garlic and sweat out the smell, they stay away. The site recommended making a garlic paste and spreading it on your skin. So that's what I did.

For the **first** time in a **long** time, I slept like a baby. The **next** morning, I went to work and found out I had a **new cute** co-worker. **Sadly**, it was **clear** to me that she thought she was being tortured by the **strong** smell of garlic. I can't blame her. She must've noticed that the **offensive** odor was from me.

I think I'd **better** move to Iceland. I hear it's the **only** country in the world that doesn't have mosquitoes.

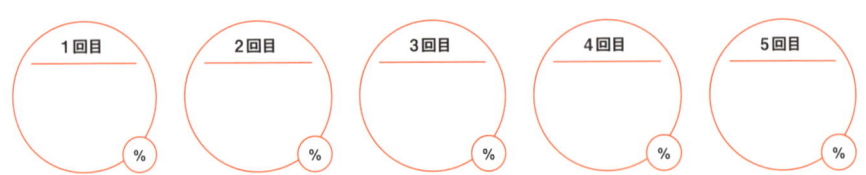

TRACK **007**, TRACK **008**

I'm sick and tired of mosquitoes!

蚊はもうイヤ！

My house is right in the middle of a busy intersection—an intersection for mosquitoes. I try to make sure all the windows are closed, but mosquitoes still get in.

One Internet site said garlic was effective. Mosquitoes are attracted to the smell of human sweat, but when you eat garlic and sweat out the smell, they stay away. The site recommended making a garlic paste and spreading it on your skin. So that's what I did.

For the first time in a long time, I slept like a baby. The next morning, I went to work and found out I had a new cute co-worker. Sadly, it was clear to me that she thought she was being tortured by the strong smell of garlic. I can't blame her. She must've noticed that the offensive odor was from me.

I think I'd better move to Iceland. I hear it's the only country in the world that doesn't have mosquitoes.

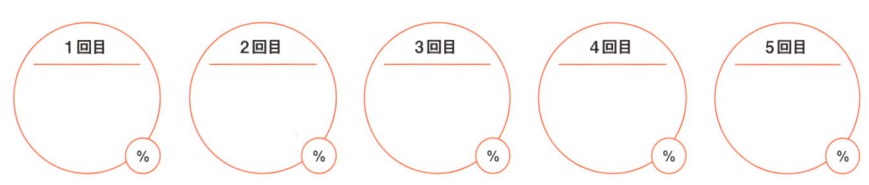

さらに英語をスラスラ読むポイント

意味がなかなか取りづらい blame

I can't blame you. という決まり文句があります。「あなたをとがめることができない」、つまり「あなたは悪くないよ」「あなたがそうしたのは当然」ということです。下の③で詳しく！

→ ここに注目

① For the first time in a long time ...（9行目）
for the first time in a long time は「長い時の中で初めて」、つまり「久しぶりに」という意味のフレーズです。He laughed out loud for the first time in a long time.「彼は久しぶりに大笑いした」のように使います。同じ意味のフレーズとして for the first time in ages があります。

② ... I slept like a baby.（9行目）
sleep like a baby「赤ん坊のように眠る」は、「熟睡する」という意味の表現の1つです。ほかに、sleep like a log「丸太のように眠る」、sleep like a rock「岩のように眠る」、sleep like a top「コマのように眠る」と言うこともできます。

③ I can't blame her.（12行目）
I can't blame her の後には for thinking she was being tortured が省略されています。I can't blame her for thinking she was being tortured.「彼女が拷問にかけられていると思ったことで彼女を責めるわけにはいかない」とは、「彼女が拷問にかけられていると思うのは当然だ」ということです。

→ 語句

sick and tired of ...：〜にすっかり飽きて
mosquito：蚊
intersection：交差点
sweat ... out：汗で〜を出す
torture：〜を苦しめる
had better ...：〜するのがよい

→ 日本語訳

　わが家は交通量の多い交差点のちょうど真ん中にあります。と言っても、蚊にとっての交差点です。窓はすべて閉めているようにしているんですが、蚊は今でも入ってきます。

　ニンニクが効果的だと、あるインターネットサイトに書いてありました。蚊は人間の汗の臭いに引き寄せられますが、ニンニクを食べてにおいを汗と一緒に出せば、寄って来ません。そのサイトのおすすめは、ニンニクのペーストをつくって肌に塗っておくことでした。それで、実際にやりました。

　久しぶりに、赤ちゃんのように眠りました。翌朝、仕事に行くと、かわいい新しい同僚がいました。悲しいことに、彼女がニンニクの強いにおいに苦しんでいるのは、明らかでした。無理はありません。ひどいにおいが私から出ていたことに気がついたに違いありません。

　アイスランドに引っ越したほうがよさそうです。蚊がいないのはその国だけだそうです。

Day 13: I can't believe I did that!

あんなことをやってしまったなんて信じられない！

I have done a lot of stupid **things** in my **life**, but what I did last week was the worst.

I really admire one of my **colleagues**. He's smart and he's a hard **worker**. He also knows how to have a good **time**. When we have company **parties**, he always tells really funny **jokes** and says witty **things**. He seems to be especially nice to me.

I was sure he wanted to get closer to me, so I decided not to wait any longer. I sent him an **e-mail**. I was hoping I would get a reply right away, but I didn't. He acted like nothing had happened, but my **boss** was different. When I was alone with him in the copy **room**, he whispered, "You're so cute," in my **ear**.

I went **home**, and then checked the **e-mail** I sent. Then I realized something—I had sent the **message** to my boss! What am I going to tell my **boss** the next time I see him?

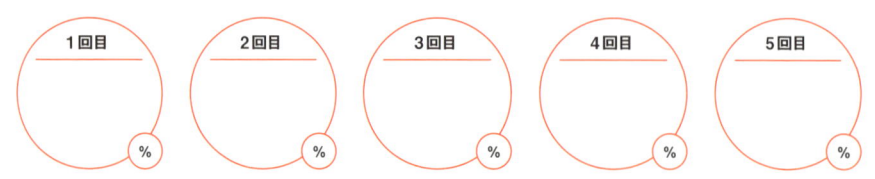

day 14
I can't believe I did that!

TRACK 009, TRACK 010

動詞に注目して音読してください

あんなことをやってしまったなんて信じられない！

I have done a lot of stupid things in my life, but what I did last week was the worst.

I really **admire** one of my colleagues. He's smart and he's a hard worker. He also **knows** how to **have** a good time. When we **have** company parties, he always **tells** really funny jokes and **says** witty things. He **seems** to be especially nice to me.

I was sure he **wanted** to get closer to me, so I **decided** not to wait any longer. I **sent** him an e-mail. I was hoping I would get a reply right away, but I didn't. He **acted** like nothing had **happened**, but my boss was different. When I was alone with him in the copy room, he **whispered**, "You're so cute," in my ear.

I **went** home, and then **checked** the e-mail I sent. Then I **realized** something—I had **sent** the message to my boss! What am I going to **tell** my boss the next time I see him?

英文読解度 （文の内容を何％くらい理解できましたか？ 理解度を入れてください）

1回目	2回目	3回目	4回目	5回目
％	％	％	％	％

day 15
I can't believe I did that!

あんなことをやってしまったなんて信じられない！

I have done a lot of **stupid** things in my life, but what I did **last** week was the worst.

I **really** admire one of my colleagues. He's **smart** and he's a **hard** worker. He also knows how to have a **good** time. When we have company parties, he **always** tells really **funny** jokes and says **witty** things. He seems to be **especially** nice to me.

I was sure he wanted to get **closer** to me, so I decided not to wait any **longer**. I sent him an e-mail. I was hoping I would get a reply **right** away, but I didn't. He acted like nothing had happened, but my boss was **different**. When I was **alone** with him in the copy room, he whispered, "You're so **cute**," in my ear.

I went home, and then checked the e-mail I sent. Then I realized something—I had sent the message to my boss! What am I going to tell my boss the **next** time I see him?

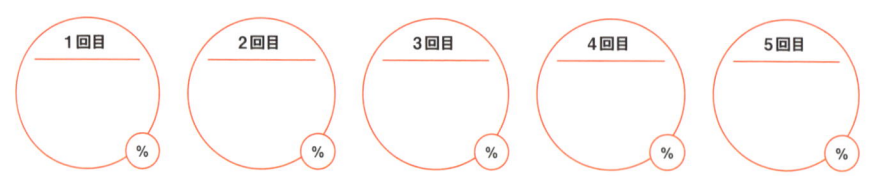

I can't believe I did that!

あんなことをやってしまったなんて信じられない！

I have done a lot of stupid things in my life, but what I did last week was the worst.

I really admire one of my colleagues. He's smart and he's a hard worker. He also knows how to have a good time. When we have company parties, he always tells really funny jokes and says witty things. He seems to be especially nice to me.

I was sure he wanted to get closer to me, so I decided not to wait any longer. I sent him an e-mail. I was hoping I would get a reply right away, but I didn't. He acted like nothing had happened, but my boss was different. When I was alone with him in the copy room, he whispered, "You're so cute," in my ear.

I went home, and then checked the e-mail I sent. Then I realized something—I had sent the message to my boss! What am I going to tell my boss the next time I see him?

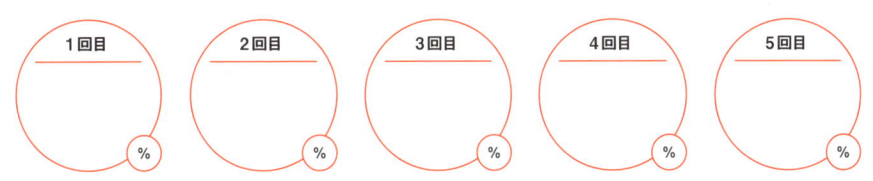

> さらに英語を
> スラスラ読む
> ポイント

なんと、形容詞と副詞の前にも置ける any

any が否定文や疑問文で名詞の前に置かれるのはよく知られていますが、この語には形容詞や副詞を修飾する用法もあります！ not ... any longer は覚えておきたいフレーズ。下の③で詳しく！

→ ここに注目

①**I have done a lot of stupid things in my life ...**（1行目）
in one's life の意味は「生まれてこのかた」です。このフレーズは、I have done a lot of stupid things in my life「私はこれまで愚かなことをたくさんやってきた」など完了形の文で使われます。また、<Never in one's life have + 主語 + 動詞>「〜は人生で一度も〜したことがない」という形でよく使われ、否定を強調することができます。

②**He also knows how to have a good time.**（4行目）
know how to have a good time は熟語と言えるものではありませんが、「楽しい時間の過ごし方を知っている」とは訳さず「遊び心がある」としておきましょう。仕事一筋ではなく、ゆとりがある人のことを言うときに使えます。

③**... I decided not to wait any longer.**（7行目）
本文にあるように、not ... any longer は「これ以上〜ない」という意味で wait とよく用いられます。「もう待てない」は I can't wait any longer. と言います。また、no longer を使うなら、I can wait no longer. とも I can no longer wait. とも言えます。not ... any longer は He doesn't live here any longer.「彼は今はもうここに住んでいない」などと「今はもう〜ない」という意味でも使われます。

→ 語句

admire：〜に感心する、〜に敬服する
witty：機知に富んだ
especially：とりわけ、特に
right away：すぐに
act like ...：〜かのように振る舞う
whisper：〜とささやく
realize：〜だと気づく

→ 日本語訳

　これまで愚かなことはいろいろやってきましたが、先週やってしまったことは最悪でした。
　非常に感心する同僚がいます。頭がよく、働き者なんです。また、遊び心があります。会社の宴会ではいつも、とてもおもしろいジョークを言ったり気の利いたことを言ったりしています。特に私にやさしいように思えます。
　彼が私ともっと近い関係になりたがっていたのは間違いないと思ったので、もう待たないことにしました。彼にメールを送りました。すぐに返信がほしいと思っていたんですが、返信はありませんでした。彼は何もなかった様子でしたが、上司は違いました。私がコピー室で上司と2人きりになったとき、彼は私の耳に「君って、とてもかわいいよ」とささやいてきました。
　帰宅して、送ったメールをチェックしました。そして、あることがわかったんです。それは、送り先が上司になっていたんです！　上司に今度会ったら何と言ったらいいの？

数字の読み方

英文中に大きな数字や、小数点が入っていたとき、読み方に戸惑う方は多いのではないでしょうか。ポイントを押さえておけばそんなことはなくなります。ここで基本的なルールを覚えておきましょう。

大きな数字はこう読む！

大きな数字が出てくると、一瞬構えてしまうかもしれませんが、ポイントは、千以上の大きな数字は「3ケタずつ区切ること」。カンマの位置を頼りに、右から1つ目のカンマが、thousand（千）、2つ目がmillion（百万）、3つ目がbillion（10億）、4つ目がtrillion（1兆）と覚えます。これを大きい順に読んでいけばOKです。

246
two hundred and forty six

3,582
three thousand five hundred and eighty two

301,000
three hundred and one thousand

年号はこう読む！

3ケタの場合は、上1ケタと下2ケタに分け、4ケタの場合はそれぞれ2ケタずつ区切ります。ただし、2000年以降は読み方が分かれており、一般的にはtwo thousand...と読みますが、従来通り2ケタずつ区切って読む人もいます。

985
nine eighty five

1985
ninety eighty five

2007
two thousand seven ／ twenty o seven

その他の数字

小数点

小数点は、小数点より手前は通常通り読み、点を"point"と発音し、それ以降は単位をつけずに読みます。

0.283
point two eight three
（小数点前のゼロは読まずに
point から読みます）

分数

分数は日本とは逆に分子（左側の数字）から読みます。分子が2以上の場合、分母は複数形になります。2の場合はhalf、4はquarterとも言います。

3/4
three fourths
（three quarters）

序数

順序を表すのが序数。世紀や記念日などの回数、第何代目などを表すときに使います。first, second, third以外には語尾に -th をつけますが、スペルが変化するものもあります。

第9
ninth（9th）

2nd Step

15日間トレーニング 2

day 1
I'm so sorry—not really!

TRACK 011, TRACK 012

本当にごめんなさい… 本心じゃないけど！

名詞に注目して音読してください

I used to date a **guy**, but one day, completely out of the **blue**, he dumped me. He said I was out of **shape**.

A couple of days later, for a **change**, I went to check out the kickboxing **gym** in my neighborhood. I was so impressed by the members' **enthusiasm** that I decided to join that **day**.

I had a hard **time** keeping up with the pace of the **workout**, but I slowly started to get used to it, and my **body** got stronger and stronger. I noticed that I was also losing **weight**. But by then, I was practicing a lot because I was having fun, not just to lose **weight**. A year later, I was in great **shape**.

Then one day, a **guy** came up to me and grabbed my **arm**. Without thinking, I kicked him hard, and he fell to the **ground**. Then I realized it was my **ex-boyfriend**!

I told him I was sorry—but in **truth**, I wasn't really sorry.

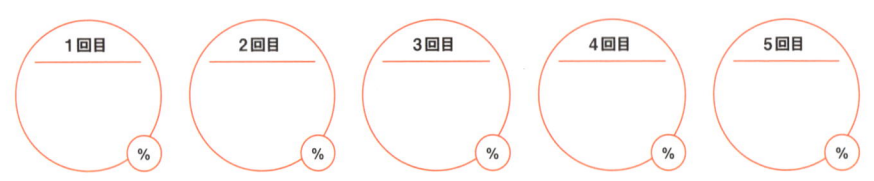

英文読解度 （文の内容を何％くらい理解できましたか？ 理解度を入れてください）

1回目	2回目	3回目	4回目	5回目
％	％	％	％	％

day 2

I'm so sorry— not really!

本当にごめんなさい… 本心じゃないけど！

動詞に注目して音読してください

TRACK 011, TRACK 012

I used to **date** a guy, but one day, completely out of the blue, he **dumped** me. He said I was out of shape.

A couple of days later, for a change, I went to **check** out the kickboxing gym in my neighborhood. I was so impressed by the members' enthusiasm that I **decided** to join that day.

I had a hard time **keeping** up with the pace of the workout, but I slowly **started** to get used to it, and my body **got** stronger and stronger. I **noticed** that I was also **losing** weight. But by then, I was **practicing** a lot because I was **having** fun, not just to **lose** weight. A year later, I was in great shape.

Then one day, a guy **came** up to me and **grabbed** my arm. Without thinking, I **kicked** him hard, and he **fell** to the ground. Then I **realized** it was my ex-boyfriend!

I **told** him I was sorry—but in truth, I wasn't really sorry.

英文読解度 (文の内容を何％くらい理解できましたか？ 理解度を入れてください)

1回目	2回目	3回目	4回目	5回目
％	％	％	％	％

day 3
I'm so sorry—not really!

本当にごめんなさい… 本心じゃないけど！

I used to date a guy, but one day, **completely** out of the blue, he dumped me. He said I was out of shape.

A couple of days **later**, for a change, I went to check out the kickboxing gym in my neighborhood. I was so impressed by the members' enthusiasm that I decided to join that day.

I had a **hard** time keeping up with the pace of the workout, but I **slowly** started to get used to it, and my body got **stronger** and stronger. I noticed that I was **also** losing weight. But by then, I was practicing a lot because I was having fun, not **just** to lose weight. A year **later**, I was in great shape.

Then one day, a guy came up to me and grabbed my arm. Without thinking, I kicked him hard, and he fell to the ground. Then I realized it was my ex-boyfriend!

I told him I was **sorry**—but in truth, I wasn't **really** sorry.

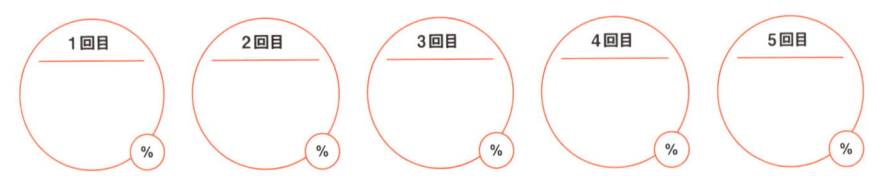

I'm so sorry— not really!

本当にごめんなさい… 本心じゃないけど！

I used to date a guy, but one day, completely out of the blue, he dumped me. He said I was out of shape.

A couple of days later, for a change, I went to check out the kickboxing gym in my neighborhood. I was so impressed by the members' enthusiasm that I decided to join that day.

I had a hard time keeping up with the pace of the workout, but I slowly started to get used to it, and my body got stronger and stronger. I noticed that I was also losing weight. But by then, I was practicing a lot because I was having fun, not just to lose weight. A year later, I was in great shape.

Then one day, a guy came up to me and grabbed my arm. Without thinking, I kicked him hard, and he fell to the ground. Then I realized it was my ex-boyfriend!

I told him I was sorry—but in truth, I wasn't really sorry.

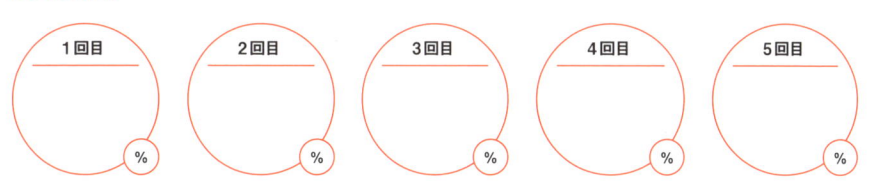

さらに英語をスラスラ読むポイント

used to とはまったく関連がない get used to

used to は「以前はよく〜した」という意味で、I used to smoke.「私は以前、タバコを吸っていた」などと使われます。このフレーズと get used to は意味も用法も全然違います。下の②で詳しく！

→ **ここに注目**

①**He said I was out of shape.**（2行目）、**... I was in great shape.**（10行目）
「スタイルがいい」は in great shape、「スタイルが悪い」は out of shape と言うことができます。shape は「（物の）形」のほかに、「（人の）体形」という意味でも用いられます。「（人の）体形」は style と言うことはできません。

②**... get used to it ...**（7行目）
get used to ... は「〜に慣れる」という意味で、名詞や動名詞（ing形）が後に続きます。ここの to は不定詞をつくる to ではないので、動詞の原形は後に続けられません。そのため、「日本の生活に慣れる」を get used to live in Japan と言うのは誤りで、正しくは get used to living in Japan です。

③**... my body got stronger and stronger.**（7行目）
<get + 比較級 + and + 比較級> で「だんだん〜になる」という意味。my body got stronger だと「私の体は（以前より）強くなった」ですが、my body got stronger and stronger は「私の体はだんだん強くなった」という意味です。

→ 語句

out of the blue：突然、いきなり
dump：〈恋人〉を捨てる
check ... out：〜を調査する
enthusiasm：熱意
have a hard time ...ing：〜するのに苦労する
workout：練習、トレーニング
lose weight：体重が減る、やせる
fall to the ground：地面に倒れる
in truth：実際は、実は

→ 日本語訳

　前に男の人と付き合っていましたが、ある日、いきなり振られたんです。スタイルが悪いと言われました。
　２日が経ち、気晴らしに近所のキックボクシング・ジムを見に行きました。そこの方々の熱意に感動して、その日に会員になることにしました。
　稽古のペースについていくのが大変でしたが、徐々に慣れていき、体がどんどん強くなりました。体重が落ちていることに気づきましたが、そのときまでは、やせることが目的ではなく、楽しいという理由でよく稽古をやっていました。１年後、スタイルがとてもよくなりました。
　そして、ある日、男の人がやって来て私の腕をつかみました。無意識に振り向き、強く蹴り、男は地面に倒れました。そのとき、それが元カレだとわかったんです！
　ごめんなさいと言ったんですが、実際はあまり悪いとは思いませんでした。

day 4
If you can't do it, just fake it.

できないことでも、できるふり

One day, as I was talking to my **friends**, we started discussing the **idea** of forming a **band**. I'm not really very musical, but I did take three guitar **lessons** in junior high, so I said I could play the **guitar**. I thought it was just **talk** anyway.

But we really did decide to get together and play some Rolling Stones **songs**. First I had to get a **guitar**. Then I got on the Internet and found a guitar **lesson**. For the next week, I played the **guitar**, ate and slept—nothing else.

When we got together and played, the other band **members** said I did okay. They also said we would try the Beatles next. I spent another **week** doing almost nothing but practicing Beatles **songs**. I managed to do okay.

I can't believe it myself, but I'm getting pretty good now. I feel a little guilty about not telling the **truth** to the other band **members**. I'm wondering if I should tell them what I've been doing behind their **backs**.

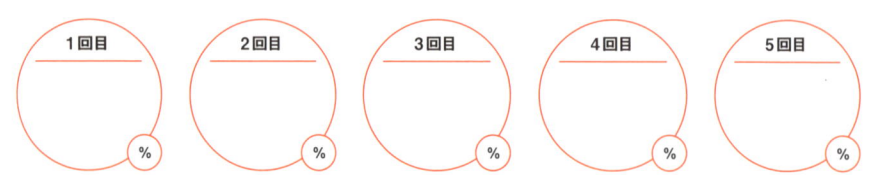

day 5
If you can't do it, just fake it.

できないことでも、できるふり

One day, as I was **talking** to my friends, we started **discussing** the idea of **forming** a band. I'm not really very musical, but I did take three guitar lessons in junior high, so I **said** I could **play** the guitar. I **thought** it was just talk anyway.

But we really did **decide** to get together and **play** some Rolling Stones songs. First I had to **get** a guitar. Then I got on the Internet and found a guitar lesson. For the next week, I **played** the guitar, **ate** and **slept**—nothing else.

When we **got** together and **played**, the other band members said I did okay. They also said we would **try** the Beatles next. I **spent** another week doing almost nothing but **practicing** Beatles songs. I **managed** to do okay.

I can't **believe** it myself, but I'm getting pretty good now. I **feel** a little guilty about not **telling** the truth to the other band members. I'm **wondering** if I should tell them what I've been doing behind their backs.

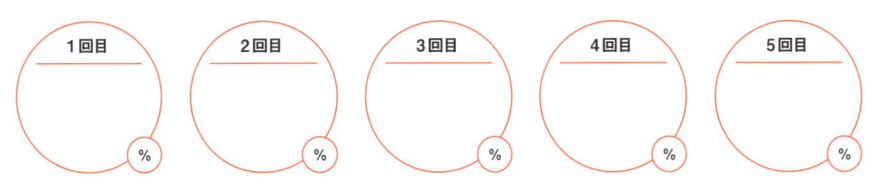

day 6
If you can't do it, just fake it.

形容詞・副詞に
注目して音読して
ください

できないことでも、できるふり

One day, as I was talking to **my** friends, we started discussing the idea of forming a band. I'm not **really** very **musical**, but I did take three guitar lessons in junior high, so I said I could play the guitar. I thought it was **just** talk anyway.

But we **really** did decide to get together and play **some** Rolling Stones songs. **First** I had to get a guitar. **Then** I got on the Internet and found a guitar lesson. For the next week, I played the guitar, ate and slept—nothing else.

When we got **together** and played, the **other** band members said I did okay. They also said we would try the Beatles **next**. I spent **another** week doing **almost** nothing but practicing Beatles songs. I managed to do okay.

I can't believe it myself, but I'm getting **pretty good** now. I feel a little **guilty** about not telling the truth to the **other** band members. I'm wondering if I should tell them what I've been doing behind their backs.

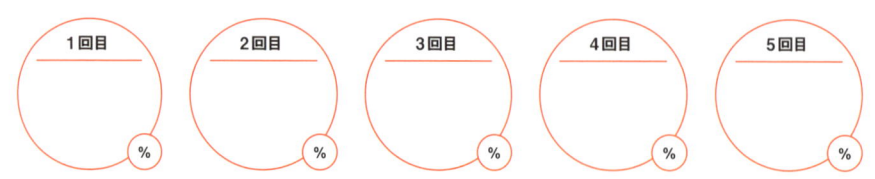

英文読解度 (文の内容を何%くらい理解できましたか？ 理解度を入れてください)

1回目	2回目	3回目	4回目	5回目
%	%	%	%	%

If you can't do it, just fake it.

できないことでも、できるふり

One day, as I was talking to my friends, we started discussing the idea of forming a band. I'm not really very musical, but I did take three guitar lessons in junior high, so I said I could play the guitar. I thought it was just talk anyway.

But we really did decide to get together and play some Rolling Stones songs. First I had to get a guitar. Then I got on the Internet and found a guitar lesson. For the next week, I played the guitar, ate and slept—nothing else.

When we got together and played, the other band members said I did okay. They also said we would try the Beatles next. I spent another week doing almost nothing but practicing Beatles songs. I managed to do okay.

I can't believe it myself, but I'm getting pretty good now. I feel a little guilty about not telling the truth to the other band members. I'm wondering if I should tell them what I've been doing behind their backs.

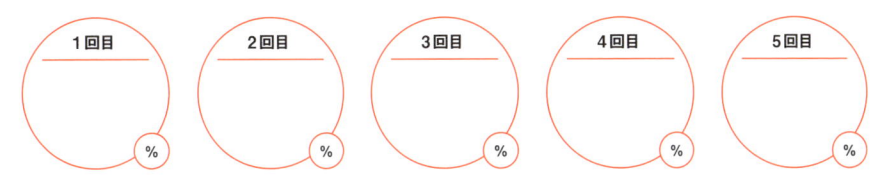

さらに英語をスラスラ読むポイント

but はいつも接続詞とは限らない

「しかし」と聞くと必ず思い出される英単語は but でしょう。英文を読んでいるときに but を「しかし」と訳して、もし意味が通じなかったら、前置詞として使われているかもしれません。下の②で詳しく！

→ **ここに注目**

① **... I got on the Internet and found a guitar lesson.**（7行目）
get on the Internet の get on は「〜につなぐ」という意味。got on the Internet and found a guitar lesson「インターネットにつなぎ、ギターのレッスンを見つけた」とは、単に「インターネットでギターのレッスンを見つけた」ということです。get on the Internet「インターネットにつなぐ」は get online とも言えます。

② **... doing almost nothing but practice Beatles songs.**（12行目）
<do nothing but + 動詞の原形>の but は、「しかし」という意味の接続詞ではなく「〜を除いて」という意味の前置詞です。直訳すると「〜することを除いて何もしない」で、つまり「〜してばかりいる」ということです。almost「ほとんど」が加わると、<do almost nothing but + 動詞の原形>「ほとんど〜してばかりいる」になります。do が動名詞（ing形）の場合は、butに続く動詞も動名詞になります。

③ **I feel a little guilty about not telling the truth ...**（15行目）
guilty は「罪悪感がある」「やましい」という意味の形容詞で、<feel guilty about + 動名詞>「〜してやましさを感じる」「〜して悪いと思う」という形でよく使われます。「〜しなくてやましさを感じる」「〜しなくて悪いと思う」と言うときは、動名詞の前に not を入れます。

→ 語句

fake it：できるふりをする
form a band：バンドを組む
musical：音楽的才能のある
anyway：ともかく
get together：集まる
manage to ...：どうにか〜する
behind 〈人〉's back：〈人〉の陰で

→ 日本語訳

　ある日、友達と話していて、バンドを組む話になりました。私は音楽の才能があまりないのですが、中学ではギターの授業を3つ取っていました。それで、ギターが弾けると言ってしまったのですが、どうせ話だけで終わるのだと思っていました。

　でも、実際に集まって、ローリング・ストーンズの曲を弾くことになりました。まずはギターを買わなければなりませんでした。そして、インターネットでギターのレッスンを見つけて、翌週は、ギターの演奏、食事、睡眠以外は何もしませんでした。

　集まって演奏したとき、他のバンドメンバーにはまあまあだと言われました。彼らは、次はビートルズの曲をやると言い出しました。私はそれからの1週間のほとんど、ビートルズの曲を練習しました。何とかうまくこなしました。

　自分でも信じられないのですが、今ではかなり上手になっています。他のバンドメンバーに本当のことを言わなくて、ちょっと悪いと思っています。彼らの知らないところでやっていることを言うべきでしょうか。

day 7
I want my friend back!

友人を取り戻したい！

I used to have a **friend** who was an **actor**. She wasn't famous, but she put her **heart** and **soul** into acting, even when she wasn't on stage.

When we were talking, she often copied a **character**. Sometimes she was a rebellious **teenager**, sometimes she was an old **lady**, and sometimes she was even a busy **businessman**. I just played along with her and enjoyed it.

When she called me, I never knew who I would be talking to. She could be a **politician**, a police **officer** or a tour **guide**.

One day, she called me and I thought she was playing a sad **girl**. She told me she had broken up with her **boyfriend**. She apologized to me for keeping it a **secret**. After talking to her for a while, I just laughed and hung up the **phone**. Since then, she never calls me and never answers my **calls**.

The other day, someone told me she really had split with her **boyfriend**. I felt terrible. How can I get my **friend** back?

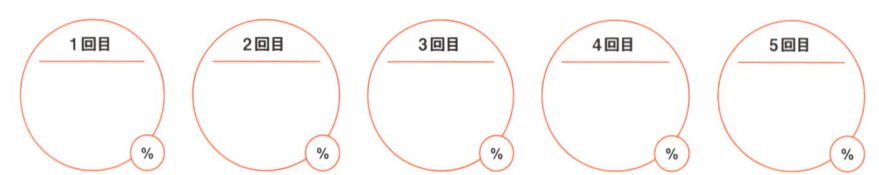

day 8 I want my friend back!

友人を取り戻したい！

I used to **have** a friend who was an actor. She wasn't famous, but she **put** her heart and soul into **acting**, even when she wasn't on stage.

When we were **talking**, she often **copied** a character. Sometimes she was a rebellious teenager, sometimes she was an old lady, and sometimes she was even a busy businessman. I just **played** along with her and **enjoyed** it.

When she **called** me, I never **knew** who I would be talking to. She could be a politician, a police officer or a tour guide.

One day, she **called** me and I **thought** she was playing a sad girl. She told me she had **broken** up with her boyfriend. She **apologized** to me for keeping it a secret. After **talking** to her for a while, I just **laughed** and **hung** up the phone. Since then, she never **calls** me and never **answers** my calls.

The other day, someone **told** me she really had **split** with her boyfriend. I **felt** terrible. How can I get my friend back?

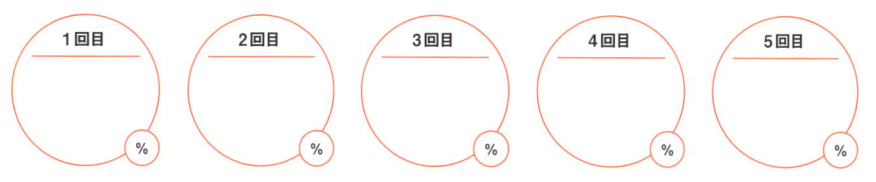

英文読解度 （文の内容を何%くらい理解できましたか？ 理解度を入れてください）

1回目　　2回目　　3回目　　4回目　　5回目
　%　　　%　　　%　　　%　　　%

day 9

I want my friend back!

友人を取り戻したい！

TRACK 015, TRACK 016

形容詞・副詞に注目して音読してください

I used to have a friend who was an actor. She wasn't **famous**, but she put her heart and soul into acting, even when she wasn't on stage.

When we were talking, she **often** copied a character. **Sometimes** she was a **rebellious** teenager, sometimes she was an **old** lady, and sometimes she was even a **busy** businessman. I **just** played along with her and enjoyed it.

When she called me, I **never** knew who I would be talking to. She could be a politician, a police officer or a tour guide.

One day, she called me and I thought she was playing a **sad** girl. She told me she had broken up with her boyfriend. She apologized to me for keeping it a secret. After talking to her for a while, I **just** laughed and hung up the phone. Since then, she **never** calls me and **never** answers my calls.

The other day, someone told me she **really** had split with her boyfriend. I felt **terrible**. How can I get my friend back?

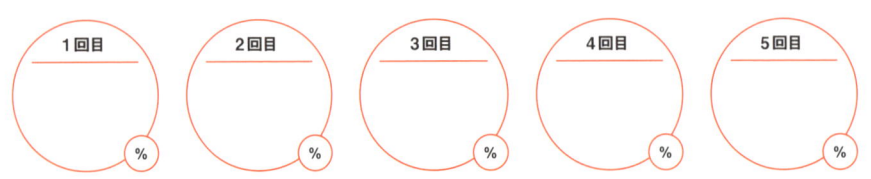

英文読解度（文の内容を何％くらい理解できましたか？ 理解度を入れてください）

1回目 ___ %   2回目 ___ %   3回目 ___ %   4回目 ___ %   5回目 ___ %

I want my friend back!

友人を取り戻したい！

I used to have a friend who was an actor. She wasn't famous, but she put her heart and soul into acting, even when she wasn't on stage.

When we were talking, she often copied a character. Sometimes she was a rebellious teenager, sometimes she was an old lady, and sometimes she was even a busy businessman. I just played along with her and enjoyed it.

When she called me, I never knew who I would be talking to. She could be a politician, a police officer or a tour guide.

One day, she called me and I thought she was playing a sad girl. She told me she had broken up with her boyfriend. She apologized to me for keeping it a secret. After talking to her for a while, I just laughed and hung up the phone. Since then, she never calls me and never answers my calls.

The other day, someone told me she really had split with her boyfriend. I felt terrible. How can I get my friend back?

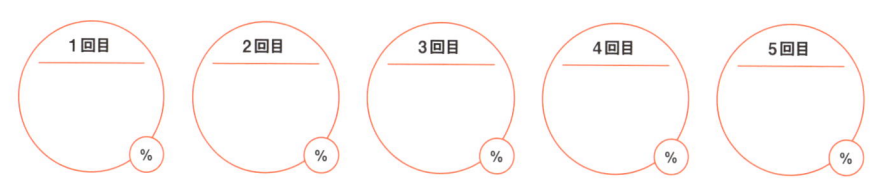

さらに英語をスラスラ読むポイント

apologizeの使い方はややこしい！

apologize「謝罪する」は、用法がちょっぴり複雑な単語です。誤って使ってしまうと、いくら真剣な謝罪の気持ちがあったとしても伝わらないかもしれないので注意しましょう。下の③で詳しく！

→ **ここに注目**

① **I used to have a friend ...**（1行目）
「以前はよく～だった」は <used to + 状態動詞の原形> と言い表します。John used to be a good boy.「ジョンは前はいい子だった」は、John was a good boy. と言ってもほぼ同じ意味になりますが、used to を使うと「今と違って以前は～だった」という気持ちを強く表せます。<used to + 動作動詞の原形> は「以前はよく～した」という意味で、I used to drink coffee.「前はコーヒーをよく飲んだ」などと使います。

② **... I never knew who I would be talking to.**（8行目）
ここの who は、ここでは talking to の目的語として用いられている疑問詞です。代わりに、「誰を」「誰に」という意味の疑問詞 whom も使えますが、who のほうが一般的です。例えば、Whom did Mary meet yesterday?「メアリーは昨日、誰に会いましたか？」は普通、Who did you meet yesterday? となります。

③ **She apologized to me for keeping it a secret.**（12行目）
<apologize to + 人 + for ...ing> は「〈人〉に～したことで謝罪する」という意味。ここの it は「男の人と出会い、2人が恋に落ちたけれど別れたこと」を意味し、どんな役にもなりきる友人はそのことを言わずにいたことを謝りました」となります。

→ 語句

want ... back：〜を取り戻したい
put one's heart and soul into ...：〜に身も心も打ち込む
be on stage：舞台に上がっている
copy：（人）をまねる
rebellious：反抗的な
along with ...：〜と一緒に
for a while：しばらくの間
hang up the phone：電話を切る
split with ...：〜と別れる
get ... back：〜を取り返す

→ 日本語訳

　役者をやっていた友人がいました。彼女は有名ではありませんでしたが、舞台に上がっていないときでも芝居に打ち込んでいました。
　彼女はしゃべっているとき、登場人物のまねをよくやっていました。反抗的なティーンエイジャーになったり、老婆になったり、忙しいビジネスマンになったりすることもありました。私はただ彼女と一緒になって楽しんでいました。
　彼女から電話があると、誰と話すことになるのか全然わかりませんでした。彼女は政治家になったり、また警察官になったり、ツアーガイドになったりすることもできました。
　ある日、彼女から電話があって、私は彼女が悲しんでいる女の子を演じているのだと思いました。ボーイフレンドと別れたと言っていました。私にそのことを黙っていたことを謝りました。しばらく彼女と話して、ただ笑って電話を切ったのですが、それからは、彼女からの電話はなく、私からかけても出てくれません。
　先日、彼女がボーイフレンドと別れたことを聞きました。心苦しくなりました。どうしたら友人を取り戻せるでしょうか？

day 10
I hope he learned his lesson.

TRACK 017, TRACK 018

名詞に注目して音読してください

もう懲りてほしい

When I was growing up, I had an unforgettable **experience**. It happened when I went to a **supermarket** with my mom at the age of six or seven. While we were shopping, I put some **candy** in my pocket. After we got home, my **mom** saw the **candy** and got really mad. She made me take it back to the store and apologize.

I had another unforgettable **experience** a month ago. I was in a fancy antique **shop** with my little son. When I was looking around, he put an old **watch** in his **pocket**. I didn't discover it until we got home.

I took him back to the antique **shop**. When I opened the **door**, I saw two police **officers** there. I was so surprised that I dropped the **watch**. Everyone looked at me; they thought I was the **shoplifter**! The owner of the **shop** yelled, "Are you coming back to rob me again?!"

My son thought it was a lot of fun to ride in the police **car**, but I hope he learned his **lesson**.

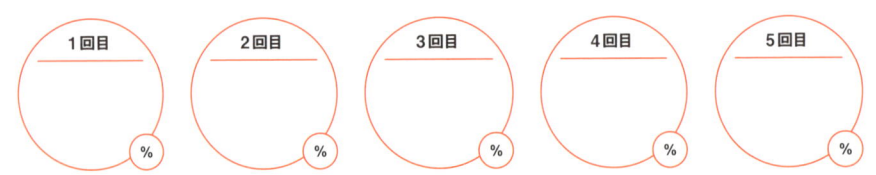

英文読解度（文の内容を何％くらい理解できましたか？ 理解度を入れてください）

1回目　　2回目　　3回目　　4回目　　5回目
　％　　　％　　　％　　　％　　　％

day 11 I hope he learned his lesson.

TRACK 017, TRACK 018

動詞に注目して音読してください

もう懲りてほしい

When I was **growing** up, I had an unforgettable experience. It **happened** when I went to a supermarket with my mom at the age of six or seven. While we were **shopping**, I put some candy in my pocket. After we **got** home, my mom **saw** the candy and got really mad. She made me **take** it back to the store and **apologize**.

I had another unforgettable experience a month ago. I was in a fancy antique shop with my little son. When I was **looking** around, he **put** an old watch in his pocket. I didn't **discover** it until we **got** home.

I took him back to the antique shop. When I **opened** the door, I **saw** two police officers there. I was so surprised that I **dropped** the watch. Everyone **looked** at me; they **thought** I was the shoplifter! The owner of the shop **yelled**, "Are you coming back to **rob** me again?!"

My son **thought** it was a lot of fun to ride in the police car, but I **hope** he learned his lesson.

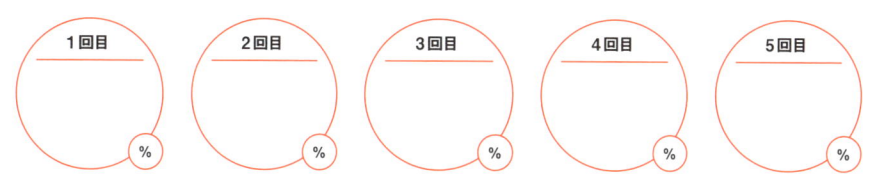

英文読解度 (文の内容を何%くらい理解できましたか？ 理解度を入れてください)

1回目	2回目	3回目	4回目	5回目
％	％	％	％	％

day 12 I hope he learned his lesson.

形容詞・副詞に注目して音読してください

もう懲りてほしい

When I was growing up, I had an **unforgettable** experience. It happened when I went to a supermarket with **my** mom at the age of six or seven. While we were shopping, I put some candy in **my** pocket. After we got home, my mom saw the candy and got **really mad**. She made me take it back to the store and apologize.

I had another **unforgettable** experience a month ago. I was in a **fancy** antique shop with my **little** son. When I was looking around, he put an old watch in his pocket. I didn't discover it until we got home.

I took him back to the antique shop. When I opened the door, I saw two police officers **there**. I was **so** surprised that I dropped the watch. Everyone looked at me; they thought I was the shoplifter! The owner of the shop yelled, "Are you coming **back** to rob me **again**?!"

My son thought it was a lot of fun to ride in the police car, but I hope he learned his lesson.

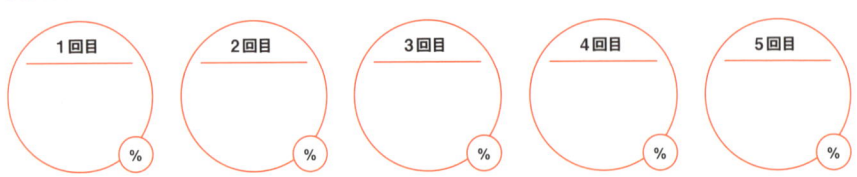

英文読解度（文の内容を何%くらい理解できましたか？ 理解度を入れてください）

1回目　　2回目　　3回目　　4回目　　5回目
　％　　　％　　　％　　　％　　　％

I hope he learned his lesson.

もう懲りてほしい

When I was growing up, I had an unforgettable experience. It happened when I went to a supermarket with my mom at the age of six or seven. While we were shopping, I put some candy in my pocket. After we got home, my mom saw the candy and got really mad. She made me take it back to the store and apologize.

I had another unforgettable experience a month ago. I was in a fancy antique shop with my little son. When I was looking around, he put an old watch in his pocket. I didn't discover it until we got home.

I took him back to the antique shop. When I opened the door, I saw two police officers there. I was so surprised that I dropped the watch. Everyone looked at me; they thought I was the shoplifter! The owner of the shop yelled, "Are you coming back to rob me again?!"

My son thought it was a lot of fun to ride in the police car, but I hope he learned his lesson.

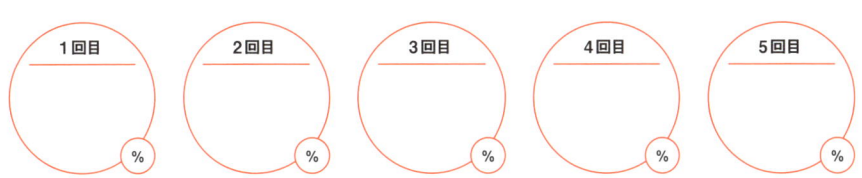

> さらに英語をスラスラ読むポイント

not...until... の意味は意訳しよう！

until「〜まで」を肯定文で使うのは難しくはありませんが、not ... until ... を直訳すると意味が取りづらくなり、「つまり、どういうこと?」と言いたくなることも。訳すときのコツは、下の②で詳しく！

→ ここに注目

① When I was growing up ... (1行目)
grow up は「成長する」「(成熟して) 大人になる」ことなので、was growing up「成長していた」は、つまり「子どもだった」ということです。余談ですが、「成長して〜になる」は grow up to be ... と言い表すことができ、「成長して医者になる」は grow up to be a doctor と言います。

② I didn't discover it until we got home. (9行目)
これは、直訳すると「私たちが帰宅するまで、私はそれを発見しなかった」となります。別の言い方だと、「私たちが帰宅して、やっと私はそれを見つけた」です。(not ...) until ... は「〜まで (〜ない)」、つまり「〜してやっと (〜する)」ということです。ここの it は前文の an old watch を指しています。

③ ... it was a lot of fun to ride in the police car ... (16行目)
ここの fun は「楽しみ」「おもしろみ」という意味の名詞です。<it is (a lot of) fun to + 動詞の原形> は「〜するのは (とても) 楽しい」という意味。a lot of fun は great fun と言い換えができます。

→ 語句

learn one's lesson：教訓を学ぶ、懲りる
unforgettable：忘れられない
experience：経験、体験
at the age of ...：〜歳のときに
fancy：高級な、豪勢な
antique shop：骨董店
police officer：警察官
shoplifter：万引きをする人
owner：持ち主、所有者
yell：大声を上げる、叫ぶ

→ 日本語訳

　子どものころ、忘れられない体験をしました。6才か7才のときに母とスーパーに行ったときのことです。買い物をしていたとき、私はポケットにキャンディを入れてしまいました。帰宅後、母はキャンディを目にして、すごく怒りました。私はキャンディを店に戻しに行かされ謝罪もさせられました。

　1カ月前にも、忘れられない体験をしました。高級骨董店に幼い息子といたときのこと。私が店内を見て回っていたとき、息子がポケットに古い腕時計を入れてしまったのです。私がそれに気づいたのは家に帰ってからでした。

　私は骨董店に息子を連れて戻りました。ドアを開けると、警察官が2人いました。私は驚いてしまい、腕時計を落としてしまいました。皆がこちらを見て、万引き犯だと思われました。店のオーナーには「また荒らしに来たのか?!」と怒鳴られました。

　パトカーに乗るのはとても楽しいものだと息子に思われてしまったのですが、もう懲りてくれたらと願っています。

day 13
I like my job, but...

仕事は好きだけど…

I like my **job**, but I hate business **trips**. I have to stay at the cheapest **hotels**.

I just got back from a four-day, three-night trip. On the first night, I stayed in a **room** with really thin **walls**. I could hear the person in the next room snoring like a **chainsaw**! I couldn't sleep, so I turned on the TV. After a while, the hotel **manager** came up to tell me that the **guy** next door had complained about me!

The next **night**, after I checked into a small **hotel**, I realized the hotel was near an **airport**. The noise from the **airplanes** was twice as loud as the **noise** from the street!

On the third **night**, I drove all the way into the **countryside** and found a quiet **hotel**. I told the **manager** not to wake me up, but at about 4:00 AM, I was awoken—this time by **roosters**!

If I work harder and my **sales** improve, I can at least stay at better **hotels**.

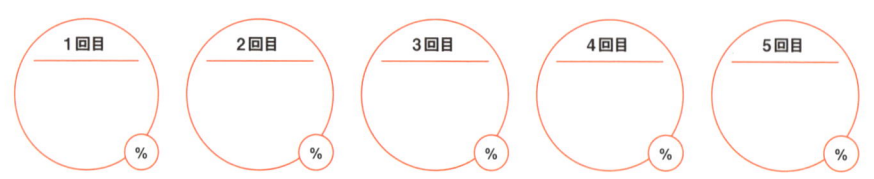

day 14

I like my job, but...

仕事は好きだけど…

動詞に注目して音読してください

I like my job, but I **hate** business trips. I have to **stay** at the cheapest hotels.

I just got back from a four-day, three-night trip. On the first night, I **stayed** in a room with really thin walls. I could **hear** the person in the next room **snoring** like a chainsaw! I couldn't **sleep**, so I turned on the TV. After a while, the hotel manager came up to **tell** me that the guy next door had **complained** about me!

The next night, after I **checked** into a small hotel, I **realized** the hotel was near an airport. The noise from the airplanes was twice as loud as the noise from the street!

On the third night, I **drove** all the way into the countryside and **found** a quiet hotel. I **told** the manager not to **wake** me up, but at about 4:00 AM, I was **awoken**—this time by roosters!

If I **work** harder and my sales **improve**, I can at least **stay** at better hotels.

英文読解度（文の内容を何%くらい理解できましたか？ 理解度を入れてください）

1回目	2回目	3回目	4回目	5回目
%	%	%	%	%

day 15
I like my job, but...

仕事は好きだけど…

I like my job, but I hate business trips. I have to stay at the **cheapest** hotels.

I **just** got back from a four-day, three-night trip. On the **first** night, I stayed in a room with **really** thin walls. I could hear the person in the **next** room snoring like a chainsaw! I couldn't sleep, so I turned on the TV. After a while, the hotel manager came up to tell me that the guy **next** door had complained about me!

The **next** night, after I checked into a **small** hotel, I realized the hotel was **near** an airport. The noise from the airplanes was **twice** as **loud** as the noise from the street!

On the **third** night, I drove **all** the way into the countryside and found a **quiet** hotel. I told the manager not to wake me up, but at **about** 4:00 AM, I was awoken—this time by roosters!

If I work **harder** and my sales improve, I can at **least** stay at **better** hotels.

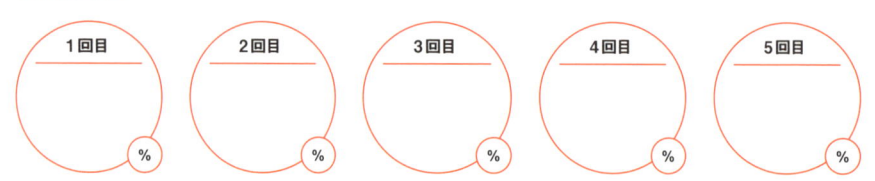

I like my job, but...

仕事は好きだけど…

I like my job, but I hate business trips. I have to stay at the cheapest hotels.

I just got back from a four-day, three-night trip. On the first night, I stayed in a room with really thin walls. I could hear the person in the next room snoring like a chainsaw! I couldn't sleep, so I turned on the TV. After a while, the hotel manager came up to tell me that the guy next door had complained about me!

The next night, after I checked into a small hotel, I realized the hotel was near an airport. The noise from the airplanes was twice as loud as the noise from the street!

On the third night, I drove all the way into the countryside and found a quiet hotel. I told the manager not to wake me up, but at about 4:00 AM, I was awoken—this time by roosters!

If I work harder and my sales improve, I can at least stay at better hotels.

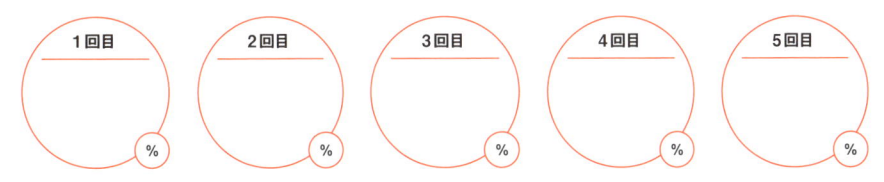

さらに英語をスラスラ読むポイント

「倍」を言い表すためのポイントがこれ！

「AはBの2倍大きい」など「○倍―」と表現する言い方はいくつかありますが、まずは「～と同じほど―」という意味の表現を使えるようになりましょう。下の②で詳しく！

→ **ここに注目**

①**I just got back from a four-day, three-night trip.**（3行目）
a ○-day, ●-night trip は「●泊○日の旅行」という意味のフレーズです。a trip of ○ days and ● nights とも言うことができます。

②**The noise from the airplanes was twice as loud as the noise from the street!**（10行目）
<as + 形容詞または副詞 + as ...> で「～と同じほど―」という意味。Janet works as hard as Bob.「ジャネットはボブと同じくらいによく働く」などと使います。<twice as + 形容詞または副詞 + as ...> となると、「～の2倍―」です。My dog is twice as big as yours.「うちの犬はあなたの犬の2倍大きい」のように使います。「3倍」であれば、twice は three times となります。

③**... I drove all the way into the countryside ...**（12行目）
drive into ... は「～へ車で行く」という意味ですが、drive all the way into ... は「～までずっと運転する」になります。ここの all the way は「(最後まで)ずっと」という意味。また、「(遠方から)はるばる」という意味もあり、遠くからやって来てくれた人に言う「ご足労ありがとう」は Thank you for coming all the way. と言い表します。

→ 語句

business trip：出張
thin：薄い
snore：いびきをかく
chainsaw：チェーンソー
after a while：しばらくたって
come up：やってくる
check into ...：〜にチェックインする
the countryside：いなか
awake：〈人〉を目覚めさせる
rooster：雄鶏
at least：少なくとも

→ 日本語訳

　仕事は好きですが、出張が嫌いです。一番安いところに宿泊しなくてはならないからです。
　3泊4日の出張からちょうど戻ったところです。初日の夜は、壁がとても薄い部屋に泊まりました。隣の部屋の人がチェーンソーのようにいびきをかいているのが聞こえました。眠れなかったのでテレビをつけました。しばらくすると、ホテルの支配人が、隣の男から私に対する苦情が出ていることを言いにやって来ました。
　次の日の夜、小さなホテルにチェックインしてから、そこが空港の近くだとわかりました。空港の騒音は道路から聞こえてきた騒音の2倍でした！
　3日目の夜は、いなかまでずっと運転し、静かなホテルを見つけました。支配人には起こさないように言っていたのですが、朝4時ごろに起こされました。このときはニワトリに！
　もっと熱心に働いて売上が上がれば、もっといいホテルに泊まることぐらいはできるでしょう。

話の流れを見抜くキーワード

単語の中には、文章のキーワードとなるものがあります。これを覚えておくと、その先の話の展開を予測できるので、より正確に英文を理解することができます。

これらのキーワードが出てきたら展開を予測！

先の展開を予測しながら読むと、英文展開の仕組みがわかり、英文理解が深まります。例えば、"Although"が出てきたら、たいてい文章は2つの節に分かれ、後ろの節は前の節とは対照的な内容になります。このように、キーワードとなる単語の後、どのような展開になるかを予測できれば、後に続く文の内容がより一層わかりやすくなります。

Although he was not so famous in Japan at that time, he now has fans throughout the world.

「彼はそのとき有名ではなかった」とありますが、Althoughがあることで、後で論旨がひっくり返ることが予測できます。

(訳)
日本ではあまり有名ではなかった彼ですが、今ではファンが世界中にいるそうです。

ほかにもこんな言い方があります！

Some people...ときたら、後半で逆の意見がくる。

Some peopleの後にはたいていbutが続き、「人は〜だが、〜は…」と逆の意見が述べられます。
Some religious people believe that the world was created in seven days, but scientists differ on this point.
(訳)信心深い人たちは世界が7日間でつくられたと信じているが、科学者たちは違った見解だ。

Of course...ときたら、後半には否定の内容がくる。

後半には否定の内容がきます。Of courseで始まる文は「もちろん〜だ」とその事実は認めながらも「でも実際は…」と否定的意見が続きます。
Of course many young baseball players would like to play in the Major Leagues, but not all can make it to the top.
(訳)多くの若者はメジャーリーグでプレイしたがっているが、全員がトップに立てるわけではない。

If you really...ときたら、後半には提案がくる。

If you reallyときたら、その後に「もし〜なら、〜をしたらどう？」と相手への提案が続きます。
If you really like greasy food, you should try the BBQ chicken pizza.
(訳)もしこってり系が好きなら、BBQチキンピザを試したら？

I know...ときたら、反対意見が述べられる。

I knowに文が続いた場合、文の内容は認めながらも、「それにしても〜だ」と反対の意見が述べられます。「わかってはいるけれど…」というニュアンス。
I know I need to go on a diet, but I love sweet things.
(訳)ダイエットをしなければいけないんだけど、甘いものには目がなくて。

おまけ

もっと上達するトレーニング

Day 1: I had a weird experience.

おかしな体験

名詞に注目して音読してください

I went to a **conference** in the United States and met a lot of nice **people** there. After the final session, a **guy** walked up to me as I was waiting for a **taxi**. He looked familiar, but I couldn't remember his **name**. After chatting for a while, he asked me where I was going next.

I told him I was going back to Japan, and suddenly his **expression** changed. He asked me, "Are you sure that's what you want to do?" I told him that I had no other **choice**. He asked me if I had told **everyone**, and I said I had. He begged me to stay longer.

Then the man got angry for some **reason**, so I was really glad when a **taxi** finally came.

After I returned to Japan, someone sent me a **picture** of the conference **attendees**. One person in the **photo** looked exactly like me! I realized that the **man** at the taxi stand had mistaken me for someone else. The **mystery** was finally solved.

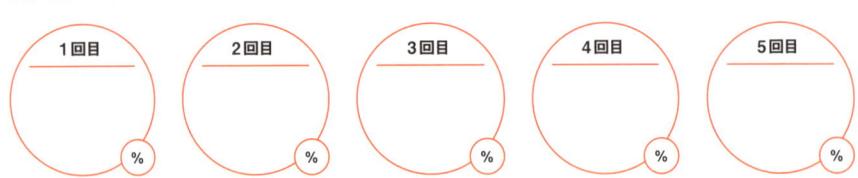

day 2

TRACK 021, TRACK 022

I had a weird experience.

動詞に注目して音読してください　おかしな体験

　I **went** to a conference in the United States and **met** a lot of nice people there. After the final session, a guy walked up to me as I was **waiting** for a taxi. He looked familiar, but I couldn't **remember** his name. After **chatting** for a while, he asked me where I was going next.

　I **told** him I was going back to Japan, and suddenly his expression **changed**. He asked me, "Are you sure that's what you want to do?" I **told** him that I had no other choice. He **asked** me if I had told everyone, and I **said** I had. He **begged** me to stay longer.

　Then the man **got** angry for some reason, so I was really glad when a taxi finally **came**.

　After I **returned** to Japan, someone **sent** me a picture of the conference attendees. One person in the photo **looked** exactly like me! I **realized** that the man at the taxi stand had **mistaken** me for someone else. The mystery was finally **solved**.

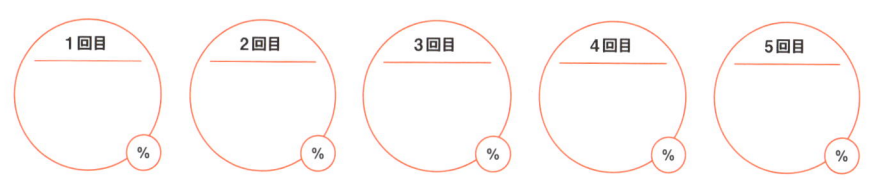

英文読解度（文の内容を何%くらい理解できましたか？　理解度を入れてください）

1回目	2回目	3回目	4回目	5回目
%	%	%	%	%

Day 3: I had a weird experience.

おかしな体験

TRACK 021, TRACK 022

I went to a conference in the United States and met a lot of **nice** people **there**. After the **final** session, a guy walked up to me as I was waiting for a taxi. He looked **familiar**, but I couldn't remember his name. After chatting for a while, he asked me where I was going **next**.

I told him I was going back to Japan, and **suddenly** his expression changed. He asked me, "Are you sure that's what you want to do?" I told him that I had no **other** choice. He asked me if I had told everyone, and I said I had. He begged me to stay **longer**.

Then the man got **angry** for some reason, so I was **really** glad when a taxi **finally** came.

After I returned to Japan, someone sent me a picture of the conference attendees. One person in the photo looked **exactly** like me! I realized that the man at the taxi stand had mistaken me for someone else. The mystery was **finally** solved.

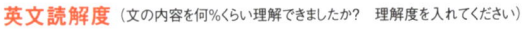

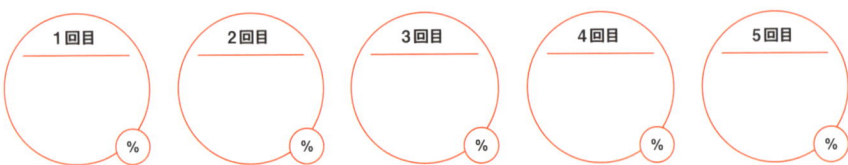

I had a weird experience.

おかしな体験

I went to a conference in the United States and met a lot of nice people there. After the final session, a guy walked up to me as I was waiting for a taxi. He looked familiar, but I couldn't remember his name. After chatting for a while, he asked me where I was going next.

I told him I was going back to Japan, and suddenly his expression changed. He asked me, "Are you sure that's what you want to do?" I told him that I had no other choice. He asked me if I had told everyone, and I said I had. He begged me to stay longer.

Then the man got angry for some reason, so I was really glad when a taxi finally came.

After I returned to Japan, someone sent me a picture of the conference attendees. One person in the photo looked exactly like me! I realized that the man at the taxi stand had mistaken me for someone else. The mystery was finally solved.

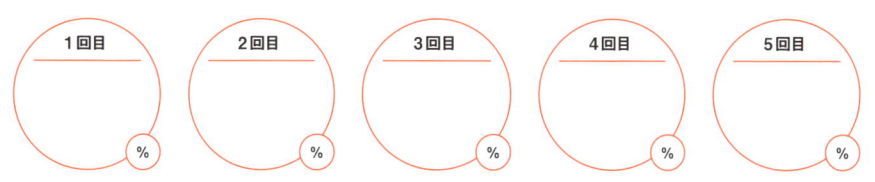

さらに英語をスラスラ読むポイント

as「〜するとき」は when に言い換えられない！

接続詞 as には「〜なので」や「〜するにつれて」、「〜するとき」などの意味があります。「〜するとき」と言えば when ですが、when と as には "ある違い" があります。下の①で詳しく！

→ ここに注目

① ... a guy walked up to me as I was waiting for a taxi.（2行目）
ここの as は 接続詞で、「〜するとき」という意味です。as は、when と異なり、出来事の同時性を強調します。ここでは、I was waiting for a taxi「私がタクシーを待っていた」ことと、a guy walked up to me「男の人が私のところにやって来た」ことが同時に起こったことが強調されています。さらに同時性を高めるためには、just as...「ちょうど〜するとき」と言います。

② He asked me if I had told everyone, and I said I had.（8行目）
ここの had 2つは、過去完了形の文で使われる had です。2つ目の後には told everyone が省略されています。過去完了形は、簡単に言うと、過去の一時点より前のことを表すのに使われます。この文では、He asked me「彼は私に聞いた」と I said「私は言った」が過去の一時点で、I had told everyone「私はみんなに言った」と I had (told everyone)「私はそうした（みんなに言った）」が過去の一時点より前のことです。

③ The mystery was finally solved.（16行目）
主人公はタクシー乗り場で男性に話しかけられ、彼の言うことが理解できずにいました。男性が話しかけてきた理由が mystery「謎」だと表現されています。この文はその「謎」が was finally solved「ようやく解けた」という意味です。

→ 語句

weird：不思議な
conference：会議
session：会合
familiar：なじみの
expression：表情、顔つき
beg：頼む、懇願する
for some reason：どういうわけか
attendee：出席者
taxi stand：タクシー乗り場
mistake + 人 + for...：〈人〉を〜と間違える

→ 日本語訳

　アメリカでの会議に行って、多くのいい人たちに出会いました。最後の会合が終わって、タクシーを待っていると、男の人が私のところにやって来ました。見覚えがあったのですが、名前が思い出せませんでした。しばらくおしゃべりをして、彼は私がこれからどこに行くのか聞いてきました。

　私が日本に帰るのだと言ったら、突然、彼の表情が変わりました。「本当にそうしたいのか」と聞かれ、そうするしかないと言いました。彼はみんなに伝えてあるのか聞いてきたので、私は伝えたと言いました。彼は、どうかもっといてほしいと頼み込んできました。

　それから、彼はどういうわけか腹を立てたので、タクシーがようやく来たときはとてもほっとしました。

　日本に戻ってから、会議の出席者が写った写真が送られてきました。その中の1人が私とそっくりでした！　私は、タクシー乗り場にいた人が私をほかの人と間違えたのだとわかりました。謎がやっと解けました。

day 4 I didn't do anything wrong, did I?

TRACK 023, TRACK 024

名詞に注目して音読してください

私は悪くないですね？

People always tell me that I look exactly like a certain big movie star. It can be really irritating.

When I go to a restaurant, strangers come up to me and ask me for my autograph. I hate to disappoint them, but I have to tell them they have the wrong person.

I recently checked into a hotel. I asked for a single room, but the friendly manager said that he would let me stay in the penthouse suite. I certainly didn't want to say no to that. When I signed in, I used my real name, but the clerk just smiled, like he knew I was trying to protect my privacy. He clearly thought I was famous.

The next morning, everyone was really cold toward me. Someone had probably checked the Internet and seen that the movie star was somewhere else and not at their hotel. But I didn't care—I got a luxury hotel room for a great price.

I've learned that there are some disadvantages to looking like a famous person, but also some advantages!

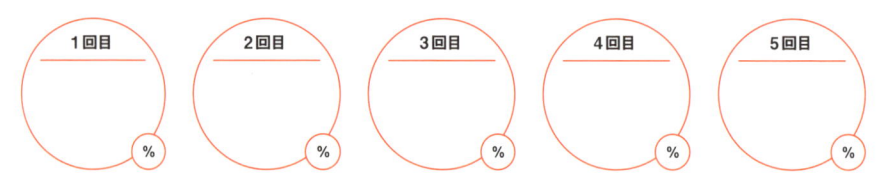

英文読解度 （文の内容を何％くらい理解できましたか？　理解度を入れてください）

1回目	2回目	3回目	4回目	5回目
％	％	％	％	％

day 5

I didn't do anything wrong, did I?

TRACK 023, TRACK 024

私は悪くないですね？

動詞に注目して音読してください

People always tell me that I **look** exactly like a certain big movie star. It can be really irritating.

When I **go** to a restaurant, strangers **come** up to me and ask me for my autograph. I **hate** to disappoint them, but I have to tell them they have the wrong person.

I recently **checked** into a hotel. I **asked** for a single room, but the friendly manager **said** that he would let me stay in the penthouse suite. I certainly didn't want to say no to that. When I **signed** in, I used my real name, but the clerk just **smiled**, like he **knew** I was trying to protect my privacy. He clearly **thought** I was famous.

The next morning, everyone was really cold toward me. Someone had probably **checked** the Internet and **seen** that the movie star was somewhere else and not at their hotel. But I didn't care—I **got** a luxury hotel room for a great price.

I've **learned** that there are some disadvantages to looking like a famous person, but also some advantages!

英文読解度 （文の内容を何％くらい理解できましたか？　理解度を入れてください）

1回目	2回目	3回目	4回目	5回目
％	％	％	％	％

day 6

I didn't do anything wrong, did I?

私は悪くないですね？

People **always** tell me that I look **exactly** like a certain big movie star. It can be **really** irritating.

When I go to a restaurant, strangers come up to me and ask me for my autograph. I hate to disappoint them, but I have to tell them they have the **wrong** person.

I **recently** checked into a hotel. I asked for a single room, but the friendly manager said that he would let me stay in the penthouse suite. I **certainly** didn't want to say no to that. When I signed in, I used my **real** name, but the clerk **just** smiled, like he knew I was trying to protect my privacy. He **clearly** thought I was **famous**.

The next morning, everyone was **really** cold toward me. Someone had **probably** checked the Internet and seen that the movie star was **somewhere** else and not at their hotel. But I didn't care—I got a luxury hotel room for a **great** price.

I've learned that there are some disadvantages to looking like a **famous** person, but also some advantages!

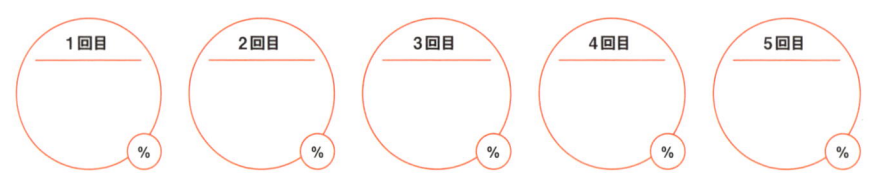

I didn't do anything wrong, did I?

私は悪くないですね？

People always tell me that I look exactly like a certain big movie star. It can be really irritating.

When I go to a restaurant, strangers come up to me and ask me for my autograph. I hate to disappoint them, but I have to tell them they have the wrong person.

I recently checked into a hotel. I asked for a single room, but the friendly manager said that he would let me stay in the penthouse suite. I certainly didn't want to say no to that. When I signed in, I used my real name, but the clerk just smiled, like he knew I was trying to protect my privacy. He clearly thought I was famous.

The next morning, everyone was really cold toward me. Someone had probably checked the Internet and seen that the movie star was somewhere else and not at their hotel. But I didn't care—I got a luxury hotel room for a great price.

I've learned that there are some disadvantages to looking like a famous person, but also some advantages!

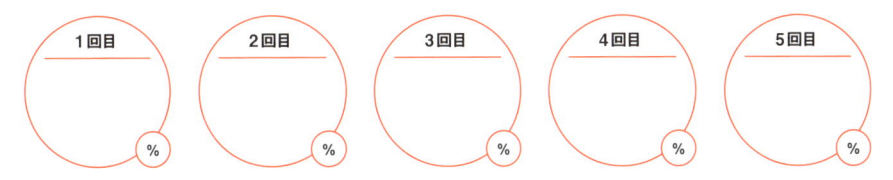

さらに英語をスラスラ読むポイント

「求める」という意味もある動詞 ask

ask は「尋ねる」という意味でよく使われますが、「求める」という意味でもよく使われます。どちらの意味で使われているか判断が難しいときは、まずは"ある前置詞"があるか探してみましょう。下の①で詳しく！

→ ここに注目

① ... and ask me for my autograph ...（3行目）
ask には使われ方がいろいろあり、そのうちの1つが <ask + 人 + for + 物>「〈人〉に〈物〉を求める」です。「彼は私に援助を求めた」なら、He asked me for my help. となります。autograph とは、有名人が色紙などに書く「サイン」です。契約書に書く「サイン」は signature と言います。sign は「標識」「合図」のことです。

② ... he would let me stay in the penthouse suite.（7行目）
<let + 人 + 動詞の原形> は「〈人〉に（したいように）〜させる」という意味。もし主人公がペントハウススイートでの宿泊を望んでいるなら、ホテルの支配人はそのスイートに泊まらせてくれるという状況です。<make + 人 + 動詞の原形> だと、「〈人〉に（無理に）〜させる」という意味です。

③ ... there are some disadvantages to looking like a famous person, but also some advantages!（16行目）
but also は「しかしまた〜も」という意味で、よく <not only + A + but also + B>「AだけでなくBも」という形で用いられます。She's not only a doctor but also a singer.「彼女は医者であり歌手でもある」のように使います。

→ 語句

have the wrong person：人違いする
penthouse suite：ペントハウススイート
sign in：署名して入る
real name：本名
protect 〈人〉's privacy：〈人〉のプライバシーを保護する
luxury：ぜいたくな
disadvantage：不利な点
advantage：利点

→ 日本語訳

　ある大物映画スターにそっくりだといつも言われます。気に障ることがあるんです。
　レストランに行くと、見知らぬ人たちがやって来てはサインを求めてきます。その人たちをがっかりさせるようで悪いのですが、人違いだと言わなければいけません。
　最近、ホテルにチェックインしたときのこと。シングルルームを頼んだのですが、親切な支配人がペントハウススイートに泊まらせてくれると言ったんです。もちろん断るなんてしたくありませんでした。署名のとき本名を使いましたが、フロント係は私がプライバシーを守ろうとしているのをわかったかのように、にこりとしました。彼は明らかに私を有名人だと思ったのです。
　翌朝、みんなの、私に対する態度がとても冷たかったです。おそらくネットをチェックした人がいて、その映画スターはほかのところにいて、ホテルにはいないということがわかったのでしょう。でも、私は気にせずにいました。高級な部屋にかなり安く泊まれたのですから。
　有名人に似ることは良いことだけでなく悪いこともあるのだと知りました！

day 7

What am I going to do?

どうしよう?

名詞に注目して音読してください

I don't like to brag about myself, but I'm a pretty good **cook**. I recently met a really nice **guy** and we started dating. After a couple of **dates**, I thought it was **time** to impress him with my cooking skills.

I spent all **day** fixing a full-course **meal** for him. When he came, I lit some **candles** to create the perfect **mood**. I wanted the night to be perfect.

The meal went as planned—until **dessert**. He had said that he liked **strawberries**, so I made him a sponge **cake** with fresh **strawberries**. After he took just a couple of **bites**, he said he'd had enough. "What?!" I said. He said he was full and couldn't eat anymore. I couldn't believe it!

We yelled at each other. I told him I never wanted to see him again, and he left. I was so angry, so to calm myself down, I decided to eat the **cake**. It tasted horrible. Somehow **vinegar** had gotten into the cake **mixture**. Now what am I going to do?!

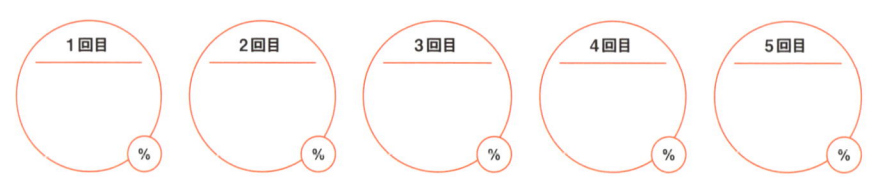

day 8

What am I going to do?

TRACK 025, TRACK 026

動詞に注目して音読してください

どうしよう？

I don't like to **brag** about myself, but I'm a pretty good cook. I recently **met** a really nice guy and we **started** dating. After a couple of dates, I thought it was time to **impress** him with my cooking skills.

I **spent** all day **fixing** a full-course meal for him. When he **came**, I lit some candles to **create** the perfect mood. I wanted the night to be perfect.

The meal **went** as planned—until dessert. He had said that he liked strawberries, so I **made** him a sponge cake with fresh strawberries. After he **took** just a couple of bites, he said he'd had enough. "What?!" I said. He said he was full and couldn't eat anymore. I couldn't **believe** it!

We **yelled** at each other. I **told** him I never wanted to see him again, and he left. I was so angry, so to calm myself down, I **decided** to eat the cake. It **tasted** horrible. Somehow vinegar had gotten into the cake mixture. Now what am I going to do?!

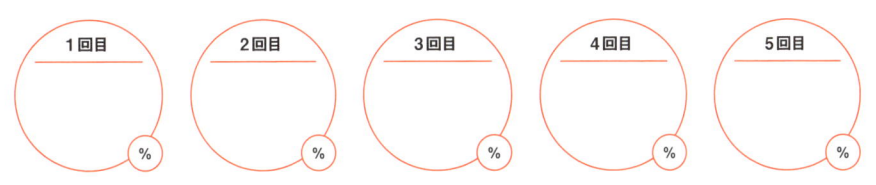

英文読解度 （文の内容を何％くらい理解できましたか？ 理解度を入れてください）

1回目	2回目	3回目	4回目	5回目
％	％	％	％	％

day 9
What am I going to do?
どうしよう?

I don't like to brag about myself, but I'm a **pretty** good cook. I **recently** met a **really** nice guy and we started dating. After a couple of dates, I thought it was time to impress him with my cooking skills.

I spent **all** day fixing a full-course meal for him. When he came, I lit some candles to create the **perfect** mood. I wanted the night to be **perfect**.

The meal went as planned—until dessert. He had said that he liked strawberries, so I made him a sponge cake with **fresh** strawberries. After he took **just** a couple of bites, he said he'd had **enough**. "What?!" I said. He said he was **full** and couldn't eat **anymore**. I couldn't believe it!

We yelled at each other. I told him I **never** wanted to see him **again**, and he left. I was so **angry**, so to calm myself **down**, I decided to eat the cake. It tasted **horrible**. **Somehow** vinegar had gotten into the cake mixture. **Now** what am I going to do?!

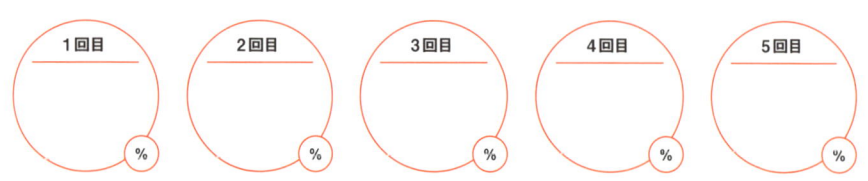

What am I going to do?

どうしよう？

I don't like to brag about myself, but I'm a pretty good cook. I recently met a really nice guy and we started dating. After a couple of dates, I thought it was time to impress him with my cooking skills.

I spent all day fixing a full-course meal for him. When he came, I lit some candles to create the perfect mood. I wanted the night to be perfect.

The meal went as planned—until dessert. He had said that he liked strawberries, so I made him a sponge cake with fresh strawberries. After he took just a couple of bites, he said he'd had enough. "What?!" I said. He said he was full and couldn't eat anymore. I couldn't believe it!

We yelled at each other. I told him I never wanted to see him again, and he left. I was so angry, so to calm myself down, I decided to eat the cake. It tasted horrible. Somehow vinegar had gotten into the cake mixture. Now what am I going to do?!

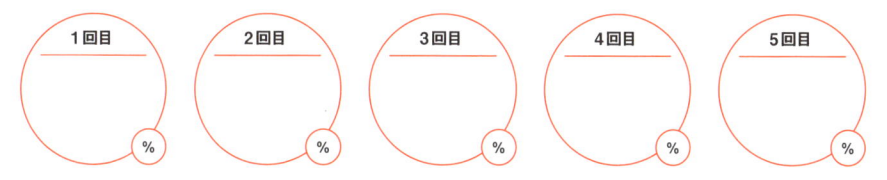

さらに英語をスラスラ読むポイント

さまざまな名詞を目的語にとる動詞 take

take は「持っていく」や「連れていく」などの意味を持つ動詞。walk を目的語にとると、take a walk「散歩する」というフレーズになります。では、take a bite はどんな意味になるでしょうか。下の②で詳しく！

→ **ここに注目**

① I don't like to brag about myself, but ...（1行目）
これは、直訳すると「私は自分のことを自慢げに言うのが好きではないが〜」となります。つまり、「自慢話はしたくないが〜」ということです。こういうことを言っておくと、自慢げに聞こえてしまうことを幾分抑えられます。

② ... he took just a couple of bites ...（10行目）
take a bite は「1口食べる」という意味。a couple of...「2つの〜」というフレーズを使えば、「2口食べる」は take a couple of bites と言い表せます。これに just「たった〜」が加わると、take just a couple of bites「たった2口食べる」になります。「〜を1口食べる」は take a bite out of ... とも、take a bite from ... とも言い表せます。

③ ... and couldn't eat anymore.（12行目）
anymore は、not など否定語を伴って「これ以上〜（ない）」という意味で、I don't work there anymore.「私はもうそこでは働いていない」などと使います。anymore は any more と書くこともできます。

→ 語句

brag：自慢げに言う
fix：〈食事や飲み物など〉をつくる
light：〜に火をつける（過去形は lit）
calm oneself down：気を落ちつける
taste ＋ 形容詞：〜な味がする
horrible：ひどい
cake mixture：ケーキ生地

→ 日本語訳

　自慢話はしたくないんですが、私は料理上手なんです。とてもすてきな男の人に最近出会って、デートするようになったんです。デートを２回したのち、料理の腕前で彼を感動させるころだと思いました。

　彼にフルコースをつくってあげるのに丸１日かけました。彼がやって来たとき、ロウソクに火をつけて完ぺきなムードをつくりました。その晩を完ぺきなものにしたかったんです。

　食事は予定通りに進んでいきました。デザートが出るまでは…。彼はイチゴが好きだと言っていたので、新鮮なイチゴでスポンジケーキをつくってあげました。たった２口食べて、もうたくさんだと言ったんです。「えっ、なに?!」と、私は言いました。お腹がいっぱいだからこれ以上は食べられないと、彼は言っていたんです。信じられませんでした！

　言い争いになりました。私は二度と会いたくないと言って、彼は出ていきました。とても腹立たしかったので、気を落ちつけようと、ケーキを食べることにしました。ひどい味でした。どうやら、酢がケーキの生地に入り込んでいたんです。さあ、どうしよう?!

day 10 I'm not a criminal!

TRACK 027, TRACK 028

名詞に注目して音読してください

私は罪を犯していませんよ！

Do you have any bad **habits**? I have a terrible habit that I can't tell **anyone** about. It's more like a **hobby**, but I can't stop—I enjoy it too much.

I work in a part of the **city** where there are a lot of department **stores** with nice **delis**. One day during lunch break, I decided to skip **lunch** and do some grocery shopping. I got a **basket** and walked around the **store**. They were giving out **samples**, so I tried them all—they tasted so good! Soon I realized I was full.

My **co-workers** bring homemade **lunches** to eat in the **office**, but I always slip out and go to one of the department **stores** nearby. I walk around pretending to be interested in buying whatever there is to sample. I don't think anyone suspects what I'm doing.

I've saved a lot of **money**, and I've tasted a lot of delicious food. I do feel kind of guilty, but sometimes I actually buy the food—well, I did once. I'm not a **criminal**... am I?

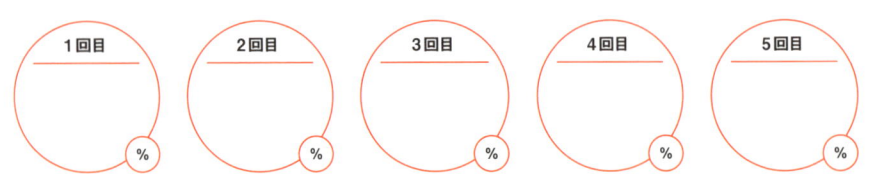

英文読解度（文の内容を何％くらい理解できましたか？　理解度を入れてください）

1回目	2回目	3回目	4回目	5回目
%	%	%	%	%

day 11
I'm not a criminal!

私は罪を犯していませんよ！

Do you **have** any bad habits? I have a terrible habit that I can't **tell** anyone about. It's more like a hobby, but I can't stop—I enjoy it too much.

I **work** in a part of the city where there are a lot of department stores with nice delis. One day during lunch break, I **decided** to skip lunch and do some grocery shopping. I **got** a basket and **walked** around the store. They were **giving** out samples, so I **tried** them all—they **tasted** so good! Soon I realized I was full.

My co-workers **bring** homemade lunches to eat in the office, but I always **slip** out and go to one of the department stores nearby. I **walk** around pretending to be interested in buying whatever there is to sample. I don't **think** anyone suspects what I'm doing.

I've **saved** a lot of money, and I've **tasted** a lot of delicious food. I do **feel** kind of guilty, but sometimes I actually **buy** the food—well, I did once. I'm not a criminal... am I?

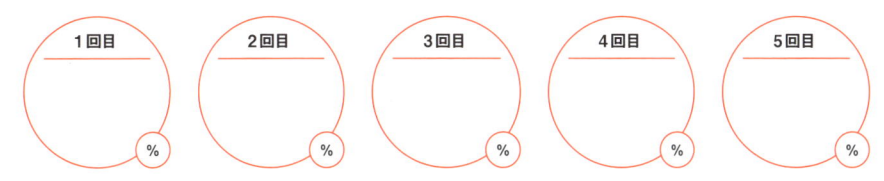

day 12: I'm not a criminal!

TRACK 027, TRACK 028

私は罪を犯していませんよ！

Do you have any **bad** habits? I have a **terrible** habit that I can't tell anyone about. It's **more** like a hobby, but I can't stop—I enjoy it too much.

I work in a part of the city where there are a lot of department stores with **nice** delis. One day during lunch break, I decided to skip lunch and do **some** grocery shopping. I got a basket and walked around the store. They were giving out samples, so I tried them all—they tasted so **good**! Soon I realized I was **full**.

My co-workers bring **homemade** lunches to eat in the office, but I **always** slip out and go to one of the department stores **nearby**. I walk around pretending to be **interested** in buying whatever there is to sample. I don't think anyone suspects what I'm doing.

I've saved a lot of money, and I've tasted a lot of **delicious** food. I do feel kind of **guilty**, but **sometimes** I **actually** buy the food—well, I did **once**. I'm not a criminal… am I?

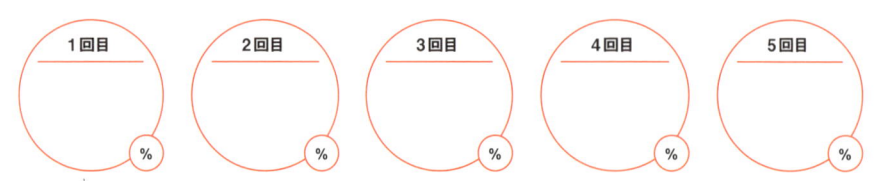

英文読解度 （文の内容を何％くらい理解できましたか？　理解度を入れてください）

1回目	2回目	3回目	4回目	5回目
％	％	％	％	％

I'm not a criminal!

私は罪を犯していませんよ！

Do you have any bad habits? I have a terrible habit that I can't tell anyone about. It's more like a hobby, but I can't stop—I enjoy it too much.

I work in a part of the city where there are a lot of department stores with nice delis. One day during lunch break, I decided to skip lunch and do some grocery shopping. I got a basket and walked around the store. They were giving out samples, so I tried them all—they tasted so good! Soon I realized I was full.

My co-workers bring homemade lunches to eat in the office, but I always slip out and go to one of the department stores nearby. I walk around pretending to be interested in buying whatever there is to sample. I don't think anyone suspects what I'm doing.

I've saved a lot of money, and I've tasted a lot of delicious food. I do feel kind of guilty, but sometimes I actually buy the food—well, I did once. I'm not a criminal... am I?

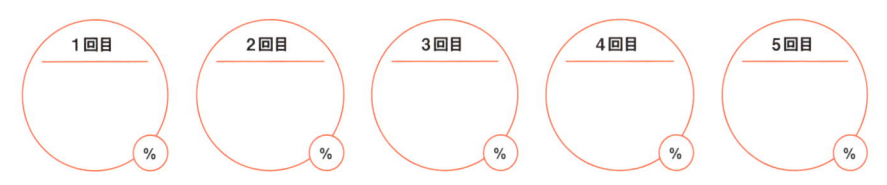

さらに英語をスラスラ読むポイント

do が助動詞として使える?!

do が動詞として使えるのは誰もが知っていますが、助動詞としても使えるのはご存じですか? Do you like apples?「りんごは好きですか」の Do は助動詞。do の助動詞用法については、下の③で詳しく!

→ ここに注目

① It's more like a hobby ...（2行目）
more like ...「むしろ〜みたいな」はよく than を伴い、〈more like + A + than + B〉「BというよりAみたいな」などと使われます。「彼女は先生というより友だちだ」は She's more like a friend than a teacher. と言うことができます。

② ... buying whatever there is to sample.（13行目）
whatever は「〜するものは何でも」、there is ... は「〜がある」、sample は「〜を試食する」という意味なので、whatever there is to sample の意味は「試食するためにあるものは何でも」、つまり「(店内に) 出ている試食品なら何でも」ということです。

③ I do feel kind of guilty ...（16行目）
ここの do は「本当に」「たしかに」という意味の助動詞で、直後の動詞を強調します。do は、主語に合わせて does になったり、時制に合わせて did になったりします。He does talk a lot.「彼は本当によくしゃべる」、I did tell John the truth.「私はジョンに本当のことを言いましたよ」などと使います。can や will など助動詞に続く動詞は必ず原形であるのと同じく、助動詞 do、does、did に続く動詞も原形です。

→ 語句

criminal：犯罪者、犯人
deli：惣菜屋、調製食品店
skip：〈食事など〉を抜かす
grocery shopping：食料の買い出し
give ... out：〜を配る、〜を配布する
slip out：こっそり去る
sample：〜を試食する
suspect：〜を疑う、〜を怪しむ

→ 日本語訳

　みなさんには悪習慣がありますか？　私には誰にも言えないひどい習慣があるんです。それはむしろ趣味と言えますが、やめられず非常に楽しんでいます。

　惣菜屋の入っているデパートが多くある地区で働いています。ある日の昼休み、昼食をとらずに食料品の買い物をすることにしました。買い物かごを手に取り、店内を歩き回りました。試食品が出されていたので、全部味見してしまいました。とてもおいしかったです。すぐに満腹感が出てきました。

　同僚は自家製の弁当を持ってきて会社で食べていますが、私はいつもそっと抜け出して、近所のデパートに行きます。出ている試食品は何でも買う様子を見せながら店内を回ります。私の行いを怪しむ人はいないと思います。

　お金をかなり節約できたり、おいしいものをたくさん味見したりしてきました。申し訳ないとはちょっとしか思っていませんが、時には実際に買ったりもします。ええと、一度だけです。私って、犯罪者じゃないですよね？

day 13 It's a small world!

世間は狭い

When I was in high **school**, I had to work part-time. After searching really hard, I finally found a coffee **shop** that would hire me.

I soon found out why they hired me—no one else wanted to work there! I worked long **hours**, but I only got paid for two hours a day. The **kitchen** area was filthy, and **bugs** and **mice** were getting into the **food**, but the boss didn't care a bit.

He was always making **mistakes** and blaming the **part-timers**. While I was there, a lot of other part-time **workers** came and went in only a few **days**, but I stayed for far too long. I was so happy when I finally finished high **school** and moved away to go to **college**.

Now I work for a magazine **publisher**. One of my **jobs** is to write restaurant **reviews**. I couldn't believe it when one day I was assigned to evaluate the coffee **shop** where I had worked. Guess what kind of **review** I wrote! It's a small **world**!

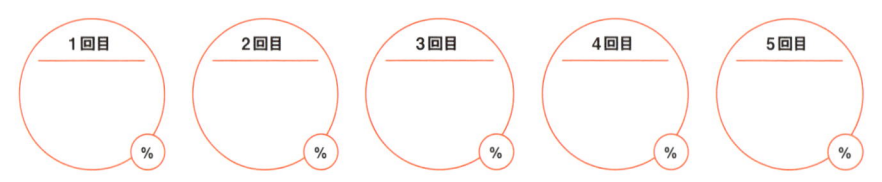

day 14: It's a small world!

TRACK 029, TRACK 030

世間は狭い

When I was in high school, I had to **work** part-time. After **searching** really hard, I finally **found** a coffee shop that would hire me.

I soon found out why they **hired** me—no one else wanted to **work** there! I worked long hours, but I only got paid for two hours a day. The kitchen area was filthy, and bugs and mice were **getting** into the food, but the boss didn't **care** a bit.

He was always **making** mistakes and blaming the part-timers. While I was there, a lot of other part-time workers **came** and **went** in only a few days, but I **stayed** for far too long. I was so happy when I finally **finished** high school and **moved** away to go to college.

Now I **work** for a magazine publisher. One of my jobs is to write restaurant reviews. I couldn't **believe** it when one day I was assigned to **evaluate** the coffee shop where I had worked. **Guess** what kind of review I wrote! It's a small world!

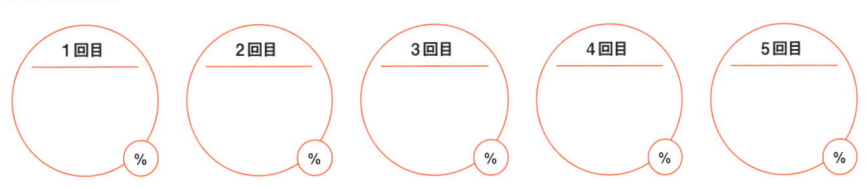

day 15 It's a small world!

世間は狭い

When I was in **high** school, I had to work part-time. After searching **really** hard, I **finally** found a coffee shop that would hire me.

I **soon** found out why they hired me—no one **else** wanted to work there! I worked **long** hours, but I **only** got paid for two hours a day. The kitchen area was **filthy**, and bugs and mice were getting into the food, but the boss didn't care a bit.

He was **always** making mistakes and blaming the part-timers. While I was **there**, a lot of **other** part-time workers came and went in only a few days, but I stayed for **far** too **long**. I was so happy when I finally finished high school and moved **away** to go to college.

Now I work for a magazine publisher. One of **my** jobs is to write restaurant reviews. I couldn't believe it when one day I was assigned to evaluate the coffee shop where I had worked. Guess what kind of review I wrote! It's a **small** world!

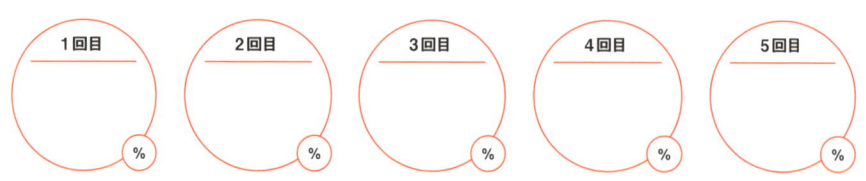

It's a small world!

世間は狭い

When I was in high school, I had to work part-time. After searching really hard, I finally found a coffee shop that would hire me.

I soon found out why they hired me—no one else wanted to work there! I worked long hours, but I only got paid for two hours a day. The kitchen area was filthy, and bugs and mice were getting into the food, but the boss didn't care a bit.

He was always making mistakes and blaming the part-timers. While I was there, a lot of other part-time workers came and went in only a few days, but I stayed for far too long. I was so happy when I finally finished high school and moved away to go to college.

Now I work for a magazine publisher. One of my jobs is to write restaurant reviews. I couldn't believe it when one day I was assigned to evaluate the coffee shop where I had worked. Guess what kind of review I wrote! It's a small world!

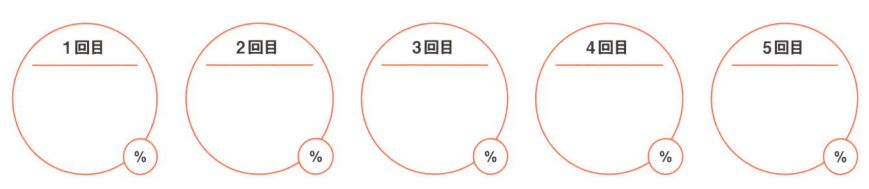

さらに英語をスラスラ読むポイント

「それ」と訳せない it の意外な用法

It's cold today.「今日は寒い」。it が日付、時間、天候状況などを述べる文の主語になると、「それ」とは訳しません。目的語として使われても、そう訳せない場合もあります。下の③で詳しく！

→ **ここに注目**

① He was always making mistakes ...（9 行目）
進行形の文で使われる always の意味は「しょっちゅう」で、何度も起こっていることを、いらだちを込めて言うときに使われます。この always は代わりに forever や continually、constantly も使われます。

② ... I stayed for far too long.（11 行目）
too の前に置かれる far は「はるかに」「大いに」という意味で、too を強調します。This shirt is far too small for me.「このシャツは私にはあまりにも小さすぎる」などと使います。

③ I couldn't believe it when ...（15 行目）
ここの it は特に何かを指しているのではなく、＜主語 + 動詞 + it + when 節／if 節＞という構文で用いられる it で、日本語には訳す必要はありません。この it は believe のほかに like や appreciate などという動詞とも使われ、I like it when I'm here.「ここにいるのが好き」、I'd appreciate it if you could hand in the report by Thursday.「木曜日までにレポートを提出していただけるとありがたいのですが」のように用います。

→ 語句

It's a small world：世間は狭い
part-time：パートタイムで
filthy：不潔な
blame：〈人〉をとがめる
review：批評記事
assign：〈人〉を（～に）配属する
evaluate：～を評価する
guess：（～かを）言い当てる

→ 日本語訳

　私が高校生のとき、私はアルバイトをしなくてはなりませんでした。必死に探して、私を雇ってくれる喫茶店がようやく見つかりました。

　雇ってくれた訳がすぐにわかりました。そこで働きたがる人がほかにはいなかったからです！　長時間労働だったのですが、バイト代は日に２時間分しか出ませんでした。キッチンエリアは不潔で、虫やネズミが食べ物に食らいついていましたが、店長はまったく気にしていませんでした。

　彼はいつも間違いを犯しては、バイトの人たちのせいにしていました。そこの店で働いていたとき、バイトのほかの人たちがわずか２、３日で大勢入ってきては辞めていきましたが、私はかなり長くいました。ようやく高校を出て、大学進学のために引っ越したときは、とてもうれしかったです。

　現在、私は雑誌出版社に勤めています。レストランの批評記事を書くことを仕事の１つとしてやっています。以前働いていた喫茶店を評価する仕事を割り当てられることになるなんて、信じられませんでした。どんな批評記事を書いたか当ててみてください！　世間は狭いですね。

CDブック

1日5分で英語脳をつくる音読ドリル

発行日　2013年3月3日　第1刷
発行日　2023年6月23日　第7刷

著者　デイビッド・セイン

本書プロジェクトチーム
編集統括　柿内尚文
編集担当　大西志帆
デザイン　萩原弦一郎（デジカル）
イラスト　中野きゆ美
執筆協力　齋藤剛士
編集協力　松原大輔
校正　アマプロ株式会社、中山祐子
CD制作　財団法人 英語教育協議会（ELEC）

営業統括　丸山敏生
営業推進　増尾友裕、綱脇愛、桐山敦子、相澤いづみ、寺内未来子
販売促進　池田孝一郎、石井耕平、熊切絵理、菊山清佳、山口瑞穂、
　　　　　　吉村寿美子、矢橋寛子、遠藤真知子、森田真紀、氏家和佳子
プロモーション　山田美恵、山口朋枝
講演・マネジメント事業　斎藤和佳、志水公美

編集　小林英史、栗田亘、村上芳子、大住兼正、菊地貴広、
　　　　 山田吉之、大西志帆、福田麻衣
メディア開発　池田剛、中山景、中村悟志、長野太介、入江翔子
管理部　早坂裕子、生越こずえ、本間美咲、金井昭彦
マネジメント　坂下毅
発行人　高橋克佳

発行所　株式会社アスコム
〒105-0003
東京都港区西新橋2-23-1　3東洋海事ビル
編集局　TEL：03-5425-6627
営業局　TEL：03-5425-6626　FAX：03-5425-6770

印刷・製本　広済堂ネクスト株式会社

© A TO Z Co., LTD　株式会社アスコム
Printed in Japan ISBN 978-4-7762-0776-4

本書は著作権上の保護を受けています。本書の一部あるいは全部について、
株式会社アスコムから文書による許諾を得ずに、いかなる方法によっても
無断で複写することは禁じられています。

落丁本、乱丁本は、お手数ですが小社営業部までお送りください。
送料小社負担によりお取り替えいたします。定価はカバーに表示しています。